The Highly Sensitive's Guide to the SENSORY Psychic Chakras

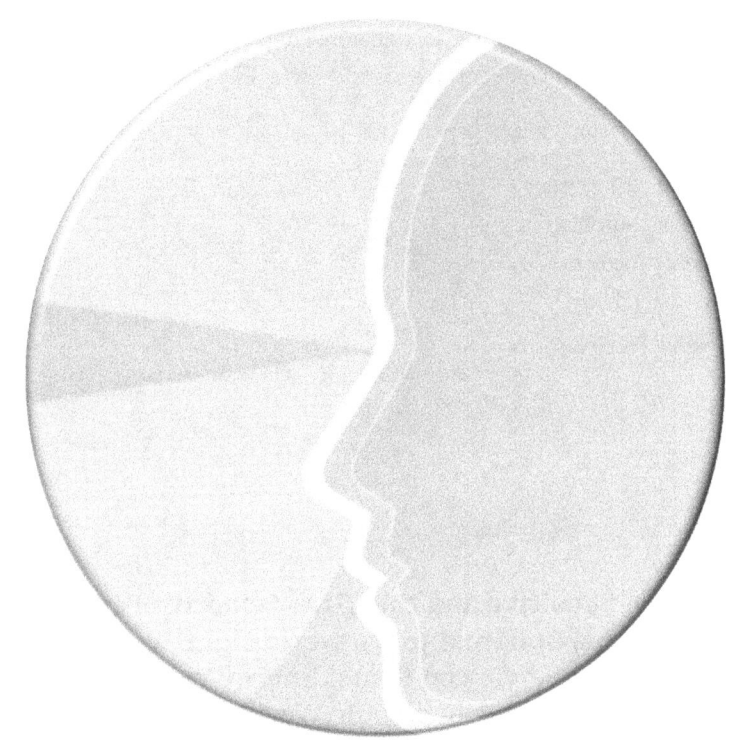

Upgrade Your Sensory Anatomy to Navigate and Succeed in a Non-Sensitive World

First Printing, **May 2017**
ISBN: 978-0-9923924-9-9
Published by Healing Knowhow Publishing,
P.O.Box 126, Toukley, NSW 2263

National Library of Australia Cataloguing-in-Publication entry:

Creator: Sri, Myra, author.

Title: The highly sensitive's guide to the sensory psychic sensory chakras : upgrade your sensory anatomy to navigate and succeed in a non-sensitive world / Myra Sri.

ISBN: 9780992392499 (paperback)

Subjects: Chakras.
Sensory stimulation.
Energy medicine.
Mind and body.
Mental healing.

For the Sensitive and the Ultra-Sensitive Person, Empaths, Spiritual Journeyers, Light Seekers, Healers, Advanced Souls, Energy Workers, Psychics, Conscious Souls Working Towards Mastery and Those Challenged by Energetic Contamination or Challenges.

NEW PSYCHIC CHAKRAS AND ANATOMY
NEW CHAKRA BALANCING FOR THE NEW ERA
The EXTRA-ORDINARY ASCENSION CHAKRAS FOR THE NEW ERA: VITAL SUBTLE BODY ANATOMY

Includes:

- Energetic Receivers
- Transducers
- Associated Etheric And Light Body Connections
- Light Channels & Filters
- Illustrations, Explanations, Protocol, Procedures

IF YOU HAVE FOUND THIS BOOK, THEN IT MAY WELL BE THAT YOU ARE READY TO BEGIN A JOURNEY LIKE NO OTHER; ONE THAT WILL TAKE YOU INTO A NEW KNOWING OF YOURSELF AND OF YOUR ENERGETIC AND SUBTLE BODY ANATOMY

APPLICATIONS FOR TIME PERIOD 2000 to 2070

By MYRA SRI – TEACHER, VIBRATIONAL ENERGY THERAPIST, SOUL and SPIRITUAL HEALER

COPYRIGHT, LEGAL NOTICE & DISCLAIMER

This material is Copyright and was first revealed in 2006 and has been taught in workshops since 2008.

The information in this document has been channelled by the Author, Myra Sri and further confirmed by a variety of reliable, spiritual and psychically gifted sources and clairvoyants. Encouragement to bring this information to the attention of evolving and evolved Souls, Light-Bringers and other LightSeekers has urged the creation of this book. Kindly please honour the time, work and effort in channelling, producing, collating, editing, researching and confirming this material and developing it into a useable form.

Therefore no copying, selling, re-distributing, re-packaging or sharing of this material is allowed without written permission or arrangement by the author. All reference to this material *must* include reference to the author.

All due care has been taken to be entirely accurate, and as much as it is in the writer's power, all currently known aspects have been addressed.

It is advisable to heed any medical advice if under current medical supervision and also to use common sense. The information contained in these writings should not be substituted for addressing physical problems appropriately, but rather hope to serve as a support for existing problems to a speedier conclusion and resolution on an energetic level.

DEDICATIONS:

Thank you to all of my students and their encouragement to release this to the world. Particularly to those gracious Clairvoyants and Spiritual Teachers that insisted that the information was spot on those occasions I doubted myself.

Especial thanks to Leonie A David, Medical Intuitive and Spiritual Clairvoyant for your support and encouragement.

Books By The Same Author
Energy Healing Secrets Series

Secrets Beyond Aromatherapy – Colour Codes Essential Oils

Secrets Behind Energy Fields – Become your own Energy Guru

Secret Truths to Health and Well-Being – Beyond Nutrition

The New Crystal Codes – Align to the New Incoming Energies

Secrets to Serene Space – The Art of Space Clearing

The New Evolved Chakras – New Era Chakra Balancing

Guided Meditations at

Some Book Reviews:

"Thrilled with the content of this book and I have read almost every aromatherapy book there is"

"I wonder why this book is not used as a textbook"

"Thanks to this eBook, I am teaching myself to rise above the conflict at work… these life skills are priceless!"

"This is an excellent, practical, down to earth book that is filled with simple techniques to get in touch with yourself, your own energy, what is affecting it and then how to do something about it."

"I found this book very informative and the techniques were simple and easy to follow. I would recommend it to anyone who does energy work.

Contents

COPYRIGHT, LEGAL NOTICE & DISCLAIMER 4
MESSAGE TO LIGHT-BRINGERS 11

INTRODUCTION 13

NEW EVOLVED PSYCHIC ANATOMY 15
   Sensitive Trap 16
   Boundaries 18

SHIFTS AND CHANGES 22
   Navigating With New Tools 24
   Quantum Mechanics and the Ancient Mystery 26
   LightWorkers or LightBringers? 27

OVERVIEW 29
   Agenda 29

NEW EVOLVED PSYCHIC ANATOMY 35
   Spiritual and Psychic 36
   Old School Psychic Structure 39
   Psychic Anatomy? 40
   The New Sensory Psychic Chakras Model 42
   What is a Chakra? 43
   The Psychic Body Matrix 46
   The Psychic Body and Its Purpose 48

PSYCHIC BODY BASICS 51

THINGS THAT CAN GO WRONG 55
   New World Problems 55
   New Era Energies 56
   What Can Affect Us 59

PSYCHIC CHAKRAS; HEAD ANATOMY 87
   The Antennae, Psychic Horns, Horn Antennae ... 89
   Transpersonal Chakra 93
   Causal Chakra 95
   Third Eye Chakras 96
   Eye Chakras 97
   Eyes & Eye Hooks 99
   Ear Chakras 102
   Nose and Mouth Chakras 104
   Nose Chakra 104

Mouth Chakra 105
Throat Chakra 106
Shoulder Transducers Chakras 106

PSYCHIC HEAD CHAKRAS 107
Psychic Centres; The Brain 108
PSYCHIC GATEWAY 113
PSYCHIC CONTROL CENTRE 115

PSYCHIC CHAKRAS; THE BODY 117
The Throat Connection Point 119
Thymus Chakra 119
CORE STAR CONNECTION POINT, ... 120
The Navel Connection Point 120

MASTER GATEWAY CHAKRAS 121
CARE With Energy Input!! 123
Buyer Beware 124
Incompatible Energies 125
Shoulder Transducers Chakras 127
Spatial Chakras 129
Mid-Shins Chakras 130
Psychic Body Chakra Links – Connection Points 131

SUMMARY - Psychic Body Chakra List 137

WORKING WITH THE NEW CHAKRAS 141
Preparing to work with the New Chakras 142
Clear the Light Channels 143
Psychic Body CORE Foundation 144
Balance & Calibrate the Psychic Body 147
Soul Registration 149

TOOLS for Working with the New Chakras 151
Psychic CORE Toner Exercise 154
LIGHT CHANNELs 157
Recommended Essential Oils 160
Other Vibrational Essences 162

AFFIRMATIONS: 163
Soul Healing Registration 163
Clearing Affirmations 164
Psychic Chakra Affirmations 166
General Affirmation Ideas 167

- Lessons from Case Histories. 168
- PRIMARY POINTS 171
  - Sensitives and Empaths... 171
  - Empaths... 174
  - Psychics 175
  - Advanced Souls, Spiritual Journeyers...................... 176
  - The Conscious, Aware and Challenged 176
  - Light Seekers and Mastery 177
- BALANCING THE CHAKRAS 181
  - BALANCE OR CORRECTION SHEET 183
- TOWARD EVOLUTION NOT EGO................................... 185
- PUTTING IT ALL TOGETHER 191
- Further Information 193
  - About the Author 195
  - THE NEW EVOLVED CHAKRAS................................. 196

MESSAGE TO LIGHT-BRINGERS

I was born an Indigo Sensitive to a family that had no clue as to what to do with me. This was the start of a very confusing journey until I eventually revoked the codes and programs placed on me by family. If not for my own Soul and my early Guides I would not have survived till now. So whenever I use the term "we" this is in acknowledgement to other than just my own intellect and includes these higher ancient aspects.

Today we find many StarSeeds and old Souls here to witness or assist in this changeover time indicated by the Mayan Calendar and other ancients. New Soul generations such as the Indigos, Crystal and Alabaster Children are entering this realm, and thus it is important to understand how to navigate these current New Era energies now and into the foreseeable future. The Sensitives are the spiritual canaries of this world; they warn of the detrimental and sing of the positive.

The discoveries of the New Chakra Systems came as a wonderful surprise to me; answers to some of my questions on healing for these times.

One of my energy skills has been the ability to be more grounded or earth connected than others when performing spiritual healing or exercises. Maybe this is what allowed my working with these energies.

Many people today are undergoing numberous changes, and as their destiny unfolds and their Soul evolves, their subtle body anatomy also has the potential to develop and mature. This then leads to **more** *unfolding and developing, until the correct energy crescendo is reached for their elevation to another level, dimension or plane, in whatever form that may take.*

We are about to go on a journey.

We will track, re-member and redefine the forgotten, lost, emerging, inherent and new evolving light pathways and energy centres and their energy body connections for a new way of being on this planet, and for a new way of managing our own personal journey and evolution.

We will clear, clean, discover, activate, align and embrace our new Sensory and Psychic anatomy.

We will share solutions to some of the practical problems plaguing the Sensitive, the healer and the journeyer.

We will enhance function and capacity to be all that we can be in this present age.

We will do all of this elegantly.

*Even just observing an **image** in one of the New Chakra manuals has activated the Initiate and assisted in their connection and alignment process! Visual connection via the Psychic Chakras in the Eyes can trigger immediate recognitions!*

So to Sensitives, True LightBringers, LightCarriers and LightSeekers everywhere, Blessings as you enhance and upgrade your energetic systems, Chakras and Light Bodies.

INTRODUCTION

Everyone has some form of a "Psychic Body"... and not just those who are called or considered Psychic.

The Psychic Body is a system of energy receptors that pick up information on an unseen level for inner processing. For some people it is not as evident or as pronounced as for others; those who are often labelled Sensitive. It is usually more developed in those who work a lot with intuition or a sense of Knowing, or who get flashes or insights that prove to have some truth to them.

Right now it would appear that many dormant or untrained psychic bodies are awakening. Most people are experiencing some kind of subtle difference over the last few years that they cannot explain. Whether it's some form of occasional and unaccountable dizziness, lob-sidedness, déjà vu or weird imaginings or dreams, most of us have experienced energy interference of some kind, which we are trying to make sense of through the new Chakra systems - but don't quite yet know how to activate or clear properly.

Only recently I was in session with someone who was feeling really sick in their stomach, to the point of real anxiety. It was only when the Psychic Chakras were cleaned out and I then balanced their Psychic Body Anatomy that the tense and "sick-y" feeling went, and they brightened and lightened up.

We have journeyed to a point in time when we are growing and developing, in actuality we are evolving, our esoteric and subtle energy body anatomy. And our new Chakras.

The new era we are in has heralded our new vital sensory upgrade information – timely news for:

- Advanced Souls
- Empaths
- Energy Workers
- Light Seekers
- Psychics
- Sensitives & Ultra-Sensitives
- Spiritual Journeyers
- The Conscious working toward Mastery
- Those Challenged by Energetic Contamination or Circumstances

Energy shifts can have a variety of impacts on our energetic anatomy. The subtle bodies (or light bodies or energy fields as some prefer) can often and generally take care of themselves, and repair, renew or reenergise by themselves given the right circumstances. And enough Time! However, not all of us have the luxury of being supported when things get too much for our energy systems to manage by themselves. For instance, a series of strong frequencies can engage our available free energy which then sets about dissecting, interpreting and redirecting appropriately the incoming or inherent message, data or information. Too much incoming energy can blow a Chakra circuit, or overwhelm; that's when we encounter problems...

With the current energetic turbulence, shift-ing, interference and for some, karmic tests, our existing Chakra systems have been challenged. Such unsettling frequencies can also affect the Sensory system and Chakras and the new Evolved Psychic Chakras which are now key players in the dramatic energy unfoldment; and easier to rebalance.

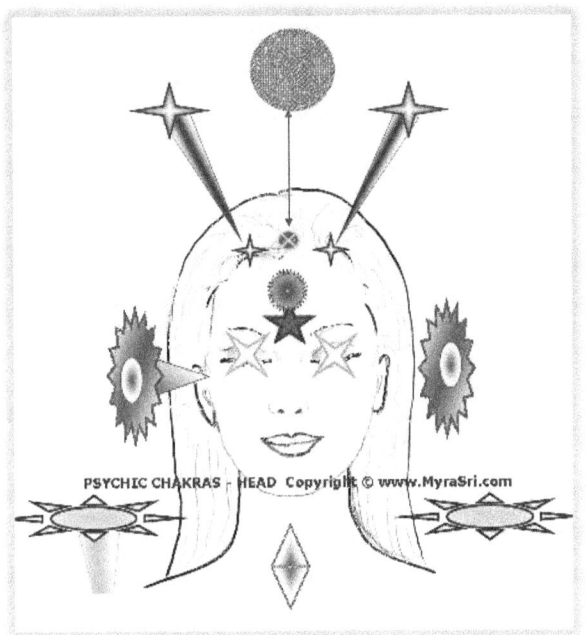

NEW EVOLVED PSYCHIC ANATOMY

The above image illustrates a section of the external Psychic Chakras and anatomy connected with the head. We will look at In-Body Chakras shortly.

Who would have thought that there could be so much activity, so much Chakra formation, so many outer accoutrements of Psychic structure around the head? Certainly not I. Not until I began my own journey into why I missed messages and why I misread signs and why I had allowed others to take advantage of me; even though I had sensed that this was not the path I should be going along...

The journey with the Psychic Chakras began initially for me around fifteen years ago in 2002 as answers started to make sense. By 2006 the picture was almost complete.

Discovering the frontal lobe attachments, the "Psychic Horns" as I call them, was the beginning of the clearing of my own psychic channels. Early on as a Kinesiologist and energy healer I had tried to clear and improve my psychic channels for greater enhancement, working with a variety of people to "switch" them on... This was not necessarily a purely selfish thing, as I had simply wanted better abilities for understanding the nature of client's issues. I tried many which ways, but still seemed to be limited to only what my physical eyes could see. Though I began to realise that I heard things – phrases, a word, a statement – and when I pursued these things, more often than not they meant something and were very relevant. Later I realised that I had some measure of clair-audience, and that it was *not* just "my imagination"...

As I cleared more, I discovered more Chakras, as I reclaimed these and listened more, more was revealed. As I trusted each revelation, I cleared some of the closing-down forced upon me as a child and by my church and regained and strengthened my abilities.

Sensitive Trap

However, I then fell into the trap of continually "looking" for answers, of continually having my mind, energy and intellect seeking the answers I was so bent on hearing. This is not a good place to be. It was almost compulsive.

I had not realised that I was an **Ultra-Sensitive**; a Highly Sensitive Being.

Being a Sensitive left me wide open to not only what I was seeking, but also whatever I encountered with it along the way. I see this with many Sensitives, and have been able to learn my own lessons from all this and to pass these lessons along.

Discovering and researching further about the new Earthing Chakras at the same time was a major benefit to the reclaiming of my own identity, abilities and place, for they assisted me in staying spiritual yet really grounded and enhanced my processing the New Era energies for positive changes and enhancements.

Each Psychic Chakra I encountered, each issue I dealt with that pointed to another Connection Point in answer to my desire to deal with whatever issue it was attached to, each step along the way brought me more information, more confirmation, more revelation. And more assurance.

I began to realise that these Chakras were not just a few addendums, a mere glossing and frosting on the energetic anatomy. This took some years of discovery; again I had to be reminded not to be consumed with continually seeking answers by energetic "investigation".

Patience was challenged, but I gained ground and understanding.

At the point of knowing most of the Psychic Chakras, I found that my psychic sensing was so open energetically that I was picking up other's thoughts about me to the extent of passing someone in the street and feeling energetically "slapped" with any negative judgements. I didn't necessarily hear their thoughts, but I certainly felt the impact.

I had learned not to seek to know what was or is going on in other's lives unless they requested a session with me, and I tried to avoid judging another as much as is possible on what I do not fully know, nor yet have been invited to investigate – Mind My Own Business...! (All part of good energetic and spiritual hygiene practise.)

Indeed I did not yet fully trust my "psychic" abilities to the degree that it could read strangers, and I had already realised that others could only probably see a small percentage of what was actually going on in my life anyway.

But this picking up of what other's felt about me, what they thought about me, it was ridiculously debilitating. I had trained my psychic awareness too much maybe?

Maybe – and maybe not...

Boundaries

What I still had to learn was the level of lack of Boundaries that I had. Protective lines of limits, borders of the being – these had been torn down by not only childhood events, abuse and violations, but also by attempts at destroying the brave light within me by those that preferred the dark. Fortunately at this time, I also began to discover some of the Survival Chakras, as I initially called them. These were Chakras that were indicated when addressing any issues to do with Survival or that pushed one into "Survival Mode"; issues that affected one's energy reserves and ability to hold onto peace. These were being discovered and revealed to me in connection with some of the debilitating issues I was still working through linked to self-worth, self-autonomy and self-empowerment. *Sensitive* had been only one part of the equation – *unsupported and abused* had been another part. The boundaries of a Sensitive can be difficult to maintain on occasion, and to have them destroyed does take some rebuilding and reclamation. But first has to come the energetic recognition.

I was also unaware of the degree of absorption of the energies of others that I had picked up over the years, particularly as a result of violence and abuse.

Lacking boundaries meant that I could be influenced by others, without even knowing that this was happening.

On a conscious level, one kind of knew where the boundaries should be; what was appropriate and what was not, what was fair and what was not. One *knew* what *not* to do to others, and subsequently expected the same treatment by others, the same considerations and respect. So then why was this happening to me, why were or had others treating me so badly?

Later hearing that we "create everything" in our lives didn't help, for truth was that only a small part of this was my own karma; *their* karma was to *do the right thing* by me *this time*, but instead they had continued their old abusive behaviour and pattern. I needed to let go of being willing to assist them in their lessons as it prevented me from moving forward in my own life and journey.

Over time I recognised and released those energies that did *not* belong to me, but that had left their own resonance in me. Dealing with these old shock resonances that signalled themselves as Survival issues led me to work with the (new) Signal-Survival Chakras. Rebuilding, indeed even recognising where a Boundary should be became very important for the continued journey and also for my improved functioning.

I had much to learn about the way energetics worked compared to rational reasoning and conscious intention – and how the subconscious could affect the actual energetic intent of a person.

As an Indigo (and Ultra) Sensitive, I had to learn that others could place labels on me that swamped my psychic anatomy; and sad to discover that certain others would try to take from me that which I knew and had worked hard to learn – simply because they could. This was usually through using their own uncontrolled or unethical psychic abilities to attempt to drain mine; whilst through ill intent caused by envy, inadequacy, laziness or greed others could try and put a stop, a claim or a drain on my abilities. I learned about these because I was forced to. And I learned to find where these things were held, and to clear them!

Someone may succeed for a short time in negatively affecting another, but when one knows what to check to ensure that there is no lingering attachment, no debilitating intent or device, no clouding or false data, then that same one can claim the final victory. And do so with a clear and ethical standing.

This then gives us our **freedom**, our **autonomy**, our **liberty** and our true **authenticity**.

This leads to self-Mastery!

Not only people, but also events can cloud our energetic anatomies. Much is happening in the world, and to those around us. Psychic Antennae and Chakras can pick up much that is going on around one – training them *not* to be so "alert" and to be able to recognise that which we need to pay attention to, and that which we need to simply note and release is *life-changing*.

Knowing my own Psychic Chakras and anatomy now allows me to monitor them, to recognise when they have been compromised, where I need to clear them, what needs repairing or rebalancing. I trust you find your answers in these pages and that this knowledge helps you (and your clients) too.

SHIFTS AND CHANGES

We are in the midst of a whole influx and sometimes storm of energies, vibrations, resonances, frequencies, messages, influences, coding broadcasts, inter-dimensional communications and more.

Some are riding it well, others are not doing too badly though they may well be feeling the chaos and sometimes the confusion, and yet others, particularly the sensitive, are very confused, or feeling quite battered and bruised energetically. Where possibly meditation used to help, or astral travel, or certain types of energy healing, much seems to have changed, and the old ways are no longer serving us quite as they once did.

In fact, whereas I once used to do some *Astral Travelling*, I no longer venture willingly or quickly into these regions, fraught as they currently are with a whole multitude of dangers. In these times of huge shifts and changes with past historic resonances also up for review, and karmic resolutions and lessons being faced by many, it is too easy and too common to encounter any one of the host of disharmonious beings and entities presently flooding the astral realms seeking resolution or revenge;

or a free ride at someone else's expense. I (and many wise others) consider that it is currently not a safe place or space to be, though this may change in the next twenty or thirty years as we emerge from and overcome the many issues being dealt with on a Planetary level and as a species, as well as a consciousness.

I have also noted that even the usual vibrational remedies had changed. For instance Essential Oils energies have shifted some of their frequencies, and their previous uses. I have found that the etheric codes and unseen colours of Essential Oils have also evolved and support newer applications and actions, and I have documented some of these in "*Secrets Beyond Aromatherapy*" at the insistence of students. We can use these codes for a variety of chakras, meridians and the new anatomy which is coming into more widespread distribution and use in the evolution of humanity.

I can share with you that all of my Crystals had to be totally reactivated in a different way as they had gone into a kind of sleep and weren't working as before. I discovered that the "old" energies were no longer as effective as they had been and that the crystals had to be reprogrammed with the new incoming energies. They are all quite happy and active again, and I marvel at their new infusion of energies now that they have been aligned with the new light and healing frequencies.

So if our usual crystalline vibrational Rescuers have met a brick wall so to speak, is it possible that they are also presenting a mirror to us that our own Auric and Crystalline system needs to be addressed and upgraded?

Yes, and I confirm that I think so.

Navigating With New Tools

To move forward with the New Era Energies, to utilise these better, to "go with the flow" if you like with the potentialities for the positive from these new energies, then we not only have to upgrade and reactivate our existing anatomy and functionality, we also have to recognise, include, connect and activate the new anatomy.

Which I think really is mind-blowingly beautiful!

It is imperative that we recognize the existing and new systems in order to better monitor, sort, clean and maintain them for optimal function. To identify one's own particular energy pathways of input and higher energy information is vital to maintaining their full functionality and clarity; and a clearer ability to navigate the huge energy shifts that we are currently experiencing. And will be doing so for some time to come.

When our psychic anatomy or chakras are clogged, then information can no longer be relied on to be clear, and can no longer be interpreted as accurate, or reliable. Psychic "madness", psychosis or "Stupidity" may be an extreme experience, but these may be caused by toxic build-up or over-stimulation. It may also be caused through damage by an inappropriate or a forced "Shakti-Pat" energy initiation or energetic transference; or some other form of Psychic Interference, Bullying or Enlistment to another's agenda. A violent Kundalini explosion / activation also has the potential to blow the psychic circuits wide-open.

One can become "punch-drunk" with energy - energetically-drunk; I have seen this happen - as they find themselves unable to correctly process or integrate the incoming information or to relate accurately to the reality they need to in order to function in present time living and participation. And one can consequently make entirely erroneous choices or decisions.

You know, it really is an exciting time. The old limiting ways are being challenged and the existing beliefs and controls are being reviewed and changed.

We have more personal responsibility than ever before, and we also have more personal Soul opportunities as well. And maybe for some, that is the very reason why they are here at this time in this place on this planet...

Quantum Mechanics and the Ancient Mystery

As we move through the incoming New Energy Waves and Frequencies, and as Global consciousness lifts to embrace Quantum Physics and Quantum Mechanics with which to temper the traditional or fixed ideas of Medicine and Religion, we are becoming more aware of our true energetic and spiritual states. Or we have the opportunity to do so.

Working with the new and evolved Psychic Body system has helped me understand how they feed into the existing Main Seven Chakra System. These are the Chakras existing within the body, mirrored by the Nervous System, and taught by the traditional Vedic, Hindu, Chinese health arts as well as various other streams of energetic healing consciousness.

Most Chakra students or practitioners use the model of the 7 Chakra System, others may use an 8 Chakra System, the main difference concerned with the Solar Plexus / Navel area. It doesn't really matter for they are both correct; for when one also studies the Hara Line System, it is easy to see how one Subtle Energy Body may appear to overlap another Subtle Body.

And some Souls are still working with past incarnations whereby their anatomy may have an overlay of a past Species, a StarSeeding, Elemental or Inter-Planetary energy system. This is not always appropriate, but it is not always dangerous, unless one has been catapulted back into the Archetype from an incarnation whilst on a Reptile planet or similar. If you come across this, we may be able to do remote work on it.

This book deals with the *Evolved Human Species* subtle body anatomy.

LightWorkers or LightBringers?

For some time I have had a problem with the term "LightWorker". Having personally been forced towards some reservations about certain "healers", "Masters" and "psychics" who claimed to be LightWorkers, but were actually far from being spiritually ethical, or indeed even working with the Light... I could still not get past the true function of the name though I now change my term to LightSeeker or LightBringer as there is quite a difference. I have met too many that count themselves as working with the Light, yet hold dark within themselves and their view of the world no matter how "positive" their speech may initially appear to be. Some are learning through their past karmic mistakes, whilst some have personal agendas running their egos and affecting their work. These I re-define as Twi-Light workers.

Balancing this new system allows so much ease in other energy Light bodies, and so much more clarity in interpreting the energetic information being pounded down to us all from The Cosmos as we ride the waves past the Mayan Long Count Calendar and the ensuing Transformational and Ascension energies. Previous knowledge has been turned on its head, and only by recognizing the shifts, waveform transmissions and the many forms of energetic vibrations do I think we can navigate with clarity and understanding through these changing times.

OVERVIEW

We will cover the Psychic Chakras in the body and that surround the body. We will also share the Connection Points within the Psychic Body itself. There are also connections with other Light Bodies that allow smooth interface to proceed between them.

We will share the **Primary Points** most affected by certain groups, i.e. the Chakras most affected by a **Highly Sensitive** may differ somewhat from those of a **trained Psychic**, or of an **energy worker**. When you have balanced and aligned all of your Psychic Chakras and the Psychic Body, it will then be simpler (and quicker) to check on your *Primary Points* when troubleshooting or rebalancing after an unsettling or negative experience or episode.

Agenda

~ Background Information to the Discoveries of the New Evolved Psychic Chakra System.

~ Current Psychic Anatomy Understanding

~ Things that can Affect the Sensitive

~ Foundations for the New Psychic Chakra Anatomy

~ Head Psychic Chakras

~ Psychic Chakras in the Body

~ Master Psychic Chakras

~ How to Calibrate the Chakras

~ Tools for Working with the Sensory Body and Chakras

This book includes Psychic Body basics and then covers the enhanced and new psychic Chakras.

Once these have been addressed, we will proceed to the In-Body Chakras and Psychic Centres in the brain and head. Then we will cover the external head Chakras.

We then work downwards to the Shoulder Chakras and other Out-of-Body Chakras and Psychic Centres till we reach the feet.

Major Psychic points – the Master Chakra Points – will be covered.

There will be a Summary Sheet of the Chakras in order from the head down.

Recommendations on Working with the New Chakras are listed. Preparation information incorporates clearing the spiritual Light Channels in the body for ease of Source / True Light connection – essential for accurate and appropriate energetic alignment particular to you and to your specific requirements on the etheric and Chakric levels. We will also look at the etheric Filters that support these channels and give suggestions. Blockages in this area will also be looked at.

Connection Points between light bodies will be listed.

There will also be recommendations for different types of issues for different groups; i.e. after initial balancing and activation Sensitives will have a list of Primary Points to check for quicker and easier Chakra clearings when they require a further follow-up or rebalance.

THE NEW SENSORY PSYCHIC ANATOMY

INCLUDES:

CURRENT PSYCHIC ANATOMY

BACKGROUND INFORMATION

PSYCHIC BODY BASICS

WHAT CAN AFFECT THE SENSORY PSYCHIC CHAKRAS

NEW EVOLVED PSYCHIC ANATOMY

The word Psychic is derived from the Greek word *psychikos* ("of the mind" or "mental") and refers in part to the human mind or psyche (ex. "psychic turmoil"). And to some degree, the mind is certainly involved.

Beginning in 2003 the evolving Psychic Body anatomy was revealing itself, or rather, I was recognising it. Since then it has become much more defined and comprehensive. The early model I had been working with, as most other energy workers I knew had, appeared to be centred around the areas that included the head - mainly the Third Eye and Crown Chakras. I then discovered a new connection at the area around or above the Navel which later proved to be the connection with the Soul Body and so this was included. I became more aware of this developing anatomy identifying itself as a new body and system. I drew little diagrams as I discovered each piece and found that working with them made a difference with clients. Over time, the head antennae was included in my diagrams though at that time I was not yet necessarily clear as to how to calibrate them to the new energies.

I also began to more fully realise the existing Psychic centres in the brain. These co-related to certain glands in the brain; the Pineal in particular which I had already been working with and in hindsight was rather obvious. The Vedics had known of these centres in the brain for some time. Further aspects of the Psychic Chakra system became clear as I questioned functionality and application of the indicated energy points on and around the body.

As this growing body of Chakras and related connections developed into a cohesive system, it became obvious to me that this was not just a series of Chakras, but a *whole system* or body governing the interpretation of invisible and vibrational information. When balanced, one could feel more of one's own energy, and find it more readily available to one's self. When unbalanced, clogged or dormant, it could enable certain difficulties, vulnerabilities or disorientation.

This was enlightening for my own balancing processes and was very helpful when I worked with Sensitives as the clearing processes settled and cleared their energy systems and helped remove overwhelm resonances.

Though in some places it is connected to and interacts with the Astral Body as well as the Soul Body, the Psychic Body has its **own** identity and functions.

Spiritual and Psychic

Most people relate to the Third Eye as the main Psychic Centre, together with the Pineal Gland. Others were and are aware of other psychic centres in the brain, and some also knew of other energy centres that were aligned with the psychic and sensory centres. However, now the assemblage of psychic anatomy has become a cohesive force and body in itself.

Considering the Chakra upgrades, knowing its structure and how it functions is now **vital** for navigating the current and prevailing energies for the foreseeable future.

Everyone has a Psychic Body to some degree or another… and not just those who are called or thought of as Psychic. The difference is that not everyone is aware of it, connected with it or able to fully use it. What is often misunderstood is the *Purpose* of this amazing anatomy...

There is some fear in certain quarters about anything labelled psychic and true psychism (psychic ability) is not necessarily understood. This is understandable to a degree, given that there have been unscrupulous people throughout history who have used their gifts for purely selfish means, regardless of being religious or not. There are also many really spiritual people that I know who are not only spiritual, ethical, moral and gifted who also possess amazing psychic abilities. To discover for myself that I had some psychic abilities, and to accept these, coming from a deeply religious background as I had, did take some time. And I had to personally see how really truly genuine and spiritual people could have these gifts and use them correctly for healing and for truth before I could dare to explore these for myself.

Anything that I came across that went against my own innate motto "Do No Harm" (a typically Christian – and Buddhist - "rule") was dismissed and left alone. I had decided long ago that I did not want to play in an energetic sandpit or playground of fear, doubt or darkness, or dabble in anything connected with spirits, dead relatives, mischievous or meddling energies of any kind, and this was my shining torch that brought what I needed to know to me.

Spiritual to me means the realisation that on some level we are all one and that what we do affects others. And that we leave a legacy behind us, and we also take one with us; and what we do returns to us in kind in some way and at some time. And Spiritual also means being responsible individually for our own spiritual journey.

Being sensitive to the pain of others had taught me much. But I had not recognised just how sensitive, empathic or psychic I was until I realised it when certain things I said – or had guessed at - actually came to pass, and that what I felt in my body was often what someone close to me was going through. All of these were lessons on life for me, but not necessarily for everyone else. When information came to me because I had asked to know, and this information was confirmed over and over and over, I was eventually able to accept that in some ways I must have some sensory abilities. I already knew that I was spiritual, so this was an interesting development.

One rule I have had for some time, is that I never use my skills unless I am asked to or unless an issue is impacting directly on me. I believe in non-infringement. One clear understanding I gained is this: a person can be spiritual and *not* psychic; a person can be psychic and *not* spiritual; or a person can be both spiritual *and* psychic. What a person *says* and what a person actually *does* will help you to decide which and what they are for yourself.

Having said all this, let us come back to what a Psychic Body – and the new evolved Psychic Body in particular - means to the ordinary person, and not just an energy worker, Sensitive or LightBringer...

What this means actually is **Autonomy** – the opportunity to filter and process information accurately in order to navigate the wealth and plethora of energies that are coming our way in these increasingly energetic and often intense times. Without infringing on another and without being infringed upon.

Old School Psychic Structure

Our current Psychic Body structure (of Psychic Centres in the body) are often based on the older versions and understandings of the esoteric and energetic information passed on by the early pioneers in the realms of esotericism, theosophy, psychism, mediumship, shamanism and channelling.

During earlier times these were discovered, explored, documented and handed down through the ages by skilled or worthy ones.

The Secret Mystery Schools of Old - such as the Temple Mystery Schools of Mithra, the early Mayan Secret Schools and Ancient Egyptian Mystery Trainings, to name a few – with their collections of many and diverse secret knowledge and understandings would have been a lot more comprehensive than our current energetic and esoteric subtle body knowledge and information. In the ancient bids for control and through programs run by fear and greed, so much has been destroyed during the ensuing wars, pirating, plundering, government overturnings and religious fanaticism that have left our knowledge base bereft in many areas. And in some cases, knowledge has been deliberately and completely obliterated and destroyed.

However, information is being revived, re-member-ed and built on. And Evolved! New windows of information are being opened. If we were to stick purely to the ancient wisdoms and information alone, we might not be prepared fully for the new waves of incoming energies. And indeed, many have come to me that now cope and navigate more completely and elegantly with their new found knowledge.

Psychic Anatomy?

We have acknowledged that there is a current Psychic system that some are familiar with, which centres around the Third Eye and /or some of the *Clair*-Skills as listed later. However, we now take into account the upgrades that have been occurring, and find we are discovering a relatively new Psychic Body anatomy that is much more than our previous "dumbed-down" five or more senses (the "Sixth-sense"). Although these senses have served us reasonably well down through the ages.

What is exciting though is what is currently occurring. For we are not only working with a variety of newer frequencies and having our current psychic structures upgraded, we have also been evolving this new psychic anatomy for this new era. New frequencies require new technology to better interpret, process, modify and utilise. New technology in this case means new anatomy.

So getting back to the current recognised systems, what *is* relatively new is the understanding that these senses, systems, structures or constructions can suffer over time through use, experiences, toxic build-up, internal pressure, global consciousness input / release and overwhelm to name a few. In short, there has been a shift as to the potential of existing psychic anatomy and furthermore, there has been an evolution process working to give us a more developed psychic anatomy and functionality. For this is required to navigate through the new frequencies and into the new Era.

The energetic shifts that began around the turn of the century and hit a kind of critical point in 2012 are still ongoing – nothing has yet settled, in fact it seems that more and more "dust" if you like, is being stirred up, and it's my opinion that mankind is actually only a part of the way through this transition from an old and stuck way of being to the path of evolution and "Ascension" as some label it.

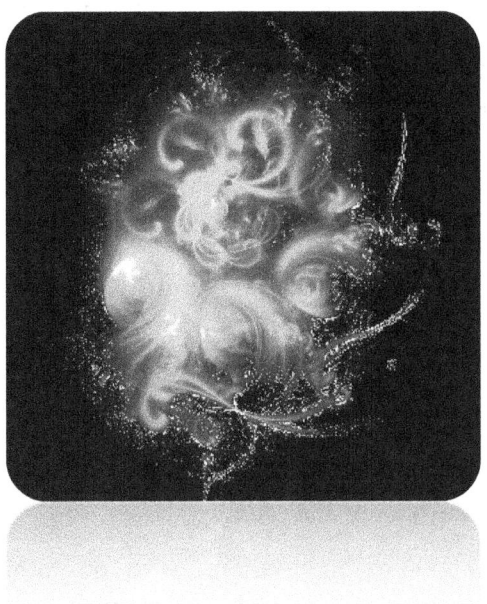

Whichever way one views our individual path to Soul freedom and the ability to follow our own true Soul purpose and destiny, much has changed and is still changing. We are still surrounded by a sort of chaos, as the new energies come through and shift and stir up "Stuff" for change, and many are busy handling both the culling of the old and the seeding or establishing of the new. And this is probably going to change again, as our Souls gain more purchase and grip with the new energies and its opportunities for growth, contribution, and personal evolution and possibly Ascension.

The New Sensory Psychic Chakras Model

The revelation that the existing model – based on the Third Eye together with in-head psychic centres and the ultra-senses (usually and generally) being fed through the Main Chakra system - was actually only a small part of the human potentiality to pick-up, receive and work with incoming energetic, vibrational and psychic information; this was an exciting and enlightening awareness for me.

Most people understand that the Third Eye is a main core psychism engine, together with a connection with the Pineal Gland in the brain. However, the new discoveries have fortunately been revealed at a time when we need it most: in a time when such a lot of subliminal and multi-levelled information and manipulation via media and a variety of other control mechanisms and methods are being used that may upset or even override our own knowing, autonomy and identity.

This new energy body differs with our other energy systems or Light Bodies, such as the Emotional Body, the Mental Body and other Auric bodies in that their outer appearance generally seems to be orbital or similar to the shape of an egg.

What is a Chakra?

As there are a good many Chakras that compose the Sensory anatomy, it is important to have some knowledge of just what a Chakra is. It is a centre of energy, a kind of wheel of light. In the body there are seven main recognised ones that spring from the Vedic understandings but which are applicable to all humans.

There are In-Body Chakras, and those that reside outside the body called Out-Of-Body Chakras. With the In-Body Chakras, there are front and back aspects, sometimes referred to as Front Chakras and Back Chakras, such as the Heart or the Solar Plexus Chakra for example. Front Chakras generally relate to what we see in front of us, what we face or is facing us, or what has come up for us to deal with right now. Generally the Back Chakras relate to what is behind us, what is in the past, buried "back there" or relating to issues with people who do not face us.

The main body Chakras are interconnected with the Nervous System, being usually placed where a group of nerve ganglions are gathered. This proximate interconnectedness allows the energy of the Chakras to sustain and support the body and its functionings.

Some Chakras can move in one direction only, clockwise or anti-clockwise, whilst some can move in both directions. The newer Cosmic energies allow for more inter-dimensional communication and interfacing, and the new Vortex energies can move in a variety of directions in order to fulfil their true functionings.

The purpose of Chakras is to receive, filter, translate, transform and to utilise Prana, Life Force, Cosmic Energy, Chi, Light and ElectroMagnetic energies in a safe and appropriate way.

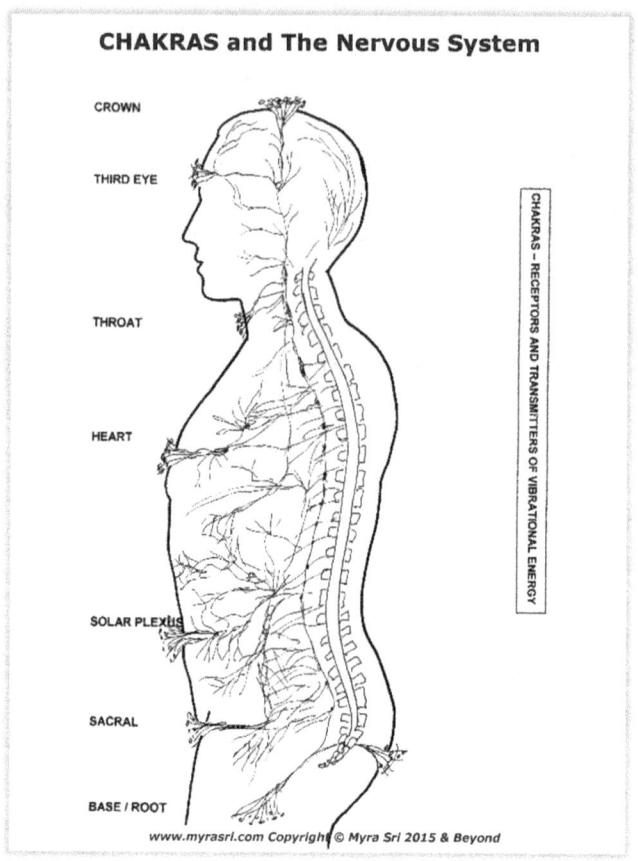

The Chakras also transmit energies, and this can be witnessed in healings, charismatic incidents, and in the supporting, projecting or controlling of outer energies and ambiences.

With the advent of the Higher Chakras above the head in the last thirty years or so, we are all granted the opportunity to connect with our spiritual nature and reclaim more easily our own Soul purpose and destiny. However, there are other Chakras that have waited to be discovered that work alongside these Higher Chakras for this new Era.

Our Sensory equipment has been updated and there are a surprising number of Out-of-Body Chakras to now support our evolution and human experience.

Chakras should be clear, spinning at the correct frequency peculiar to its function, and able to respond to external as well as internal messages easily and quickly. Otherwise they compromise health and physical and energetic functionality.

Chakras can become cloudy, twisted, disfigured, torn, bent, blocked or have a part of its anatomy loosened from its nesting place.

Repairing, clearing and rebalancing back to its correct configuration can be done by the careful, gentle, respectful and considerate practitioner. Essential Oils can assist, as can other vibrational supports such as sound, colour, essences or touch-manipulation. Balancing tools are listed in the *Tools for Working with the New Chakras* section.

And always first check if your touch energy is compatible with another's energy and Chakra before attempting energy work; there are a variety of things that can resolve Chakra damage and imbalances.

The Psychic Body Matrix

The Psychic Body does not seem to have the same Auric Egg mould or shape as the Aura and other energy fields. Looking at the Psychic Body externally, it seems to be comprised of mainly receptor sites such as the Connection Points and Chakras, though it also seems to possess a kind of gentle webbing system that flows from point to point external of the body. And this appears to me as a pale-ish green colour, almost Olive Green. The Nadis that emanate and form the greenish sheath are of fine filaments of pale green and pearly light unless they have been burned, damaged or gummed up.

I sometimes see it as a gently moving connected web with key connecting points, and at these points there is a kind of energetic sphere, even a kind of ball, or an energy torus (like a donut) with a sense of vortex energy. If you use your imagination you may see it as a form of a cloak, one that moves with the movement of information or when in an unhealthy state is "dead" feeling and clinging closer to the physical body like a matted skin – if not actually torn or ripped as I have seen in some...

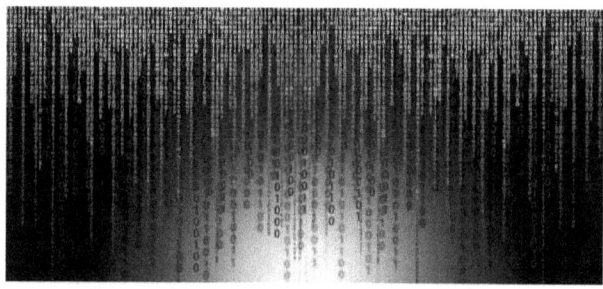

As a Matrix, it can also be viewed as having a series of Codes, which emanate from the Core and are in alignment with one's Soul Body.

The Sensory Chakras (Psychic Chakras) Matrix includes not just the anatomy we share here, but also all outstanding past history and karma. *There is more to this Matrix but too much to share in this book; and this is planned as another publication.*

The Psychic Body allows us to make better use of the new energy shifts and frequencies that we are experiencing as we move and spiral our way through the Cosmos. This new system was so large, so comprehensive that I had to call it something, and as I had not read or heard about it from any other source, I named it simply The Psychic Body.

So what exactly *is* the Psychic Body?

And just *what* is its *Purpose*?

The Psychic Body and Its Purpose

The Psychic Body is a system of energy receptors that pick up information on an unseen level for inner processing. This is to assist us in *our* own personal journey of pursuing our own particular destiny and purpose.

It is *NOT* just for Psychics; consequently working on enhancing it is *NOT* simply to make someone more psychically powerful! Rather, it helps make their work cleaner.

The Psychic Body is an enhanced communication and confirmation system. It is vital to the process of awareness and the understanding of nuances, meaning and genuineness in human and environmental interaction. And interpretation.

The Psychic Body Anatomy is comprised of Chakras and sets of Chakras, and these all relate to an overall system that is its own separate energy body. This means that there are not just Psychic Chakras, but there is an entire Psychic Body; one which receives and processes information via the major and minor psychic receptors and Primary Points placed in and around the actual physical body. Some psychic points are housed entirely within the body and others are actually contactable outside the body, which is where they receive many impressions, vibrations, incoming frequencies and interactions in the immediate vicinity and also with impressions and emanations via communication.

These external receptors connect in with and interact with the in-body receptors and interpreters to give a comprehensive internal symbolic language or image. These can confirm a situation or provide an alert as to contradiction in a given situation. Compromise, trauma damage, gumming-up through overwhelm or arrest in any of form will compromise their function, affecting a faulty interpretation of incoming and understood data and sensory information.

But this is not all...

It goes way beyond that, for it has a **spiritual purpose**, and aligning this vital energy system enhances the Soul and spiritual journey and the quality of life *on* that journey. When correctly cleared, balanced and aligned, a spin-off may be that a person's skills are safe to emerge more fully, thus enhancing their ability to interpret more correctly that which cannot be immediately seen or heard. This enhancement, though, is intended to be in the spirit of non-infringement toward others less aligned and for supporting **positive** information and change in navigating one's own life.

It is *not* for influencing or manipulating others, it is *not* for perverting to raise up or open to dark energy (and indeed the information given here is for assistance in *clearing* negative energy!), it is *not* for greed or the gathering of the resources of another. It is *not* for interfering in the minds or affairs of others, and indeed any psychic who offers up information you have *not* elicited, requested or solicited is acting unethically and does ***not*** know how to manage their abilities and is actually causing an energetic infringement. The only exception to this is in a life-or-death situation.

It ***is*** for understanding the times we live in; it *is* for recognising those things that influence or impedes our own energy, capabilities and resources and addressing these; it *is for* enhancing, complementing, benefiting and improving our path, and the paths of those that we care about or that may come to us for help.

The Psychic Body and its evolved abilities works beyond words, it works beyond what is seen, it works beyond what is heard, and it works beyond emotions. It is, in part, the reclaiming of abilities we all once possessed before language became our main form of communication. And currently it is the enhancement for us to be able to connect more spiritually in a safer and more consciously-aware way.

For some people the Psychic Chakras or Psychic Anatomy are not as evident or as pronounced as for others, such as those who are often gifted or labelled as Sensitive. It may also usually be more developed in those who work a lot with intuition or a sense of Knowing, or who get flashes or insights that prove to have some truth to them.

Right now, it would appear that many dormant or untrained Psychic Bodies are awakening in some aspect or another. Most people are experiencing forms of subtle differences over the last few years that they cannot explain. Whether it's some form of occasional and unaccountable dizziness, lob-sidedness, déjà vu or weird imaginings or dreams, most of us have experienced some kind of energy or energetic type shift or interference, which we are currently trying to make sense of through the new evolving Chakra systems, but which we don't necessarily quite yet know how to activate or clear properly.

Till now!

PSYCHIC BODY BASICS

Current Psychic Anatomy Understandings

These are the basic senses that enhanced sensory or psychic ability builds on. The normal human senses that allow us to experience the outside world are usually recognised as:

- **Sight** – light input receptors, windows to inner world
- **Hearing** – perception and interpretation of incoming sound tones and frequencies
- **Touch** – interpretation of physical stimulation or proximity, the registering of pressure, vibration, pain, pleasure, temperature
- **Taste** – registering and interpretation of sensory data via the tongue, mouth and back of the throat
- **Smell** - registering and interpretation of sensory data via the nose and olfactory nerves

Whilst the other senses or allied faculties that allow us to understand our physical place within that world are:

- **Proprioception** – whole body sensory receptor for perceptions of movement, balance and direction
- **Communication** – word-power and vocal healing (or negative) vibrations via the voice, eyes and ears

All of these faculties can also be extra sensitive, and have amplified abilities. This is where the degree of amplification makes the difference between the mundane and simply physical, with the empathic and the intuitive, through to the Sensitive and the obviously psychic. Some people can "taste" fear, some can "see" tunes, others can feel presences, but this is not necessarily recognised as being psychic, even though the skills may be just that.

So how is this ability to see, hear, feel, smell or sense-beyond the obvious-to-everybody-else happen? Just what is it that can allow this? Let us look at what we know of the Psychic senses and its anatomy to see if this gives us any answers.

Apart from the use of the Third Eye and Crown Chakras as the major tools in psychic practice, and one which has generally been associated with clairvoyance, there are other forms of psychic expertise. These provide the abilities to pick up or recognize interactions that are not of a purely 3D or physical experience or reality. Commonly working on the 4th Dimension level, some Psychics (and Sensitives) are ready to bridge to the 5th.

Those who have spent some time in exploring or experiencing phenomena, atmospherics, frequencies, ambiences, or energetic expressions not explained by the physical or the mundane will recognize the following to some greater or lesser degree:

- **Clairvoyance** – visual receiving of energetic information or phenomena
- **Clairaudience** – auditory receiving of energetic information or phenomena
- **Clairsentience** – sense reception of energetic information or phenomena
- **Clair Gustatory** – taste sensations of energetic information or phenomena
- **Clair Olfactory** – smell sensations of energetic information or phenomena
- **Auric Reception** – Astral body exploration and interpretation

- Sundry: **Chakra** input gathered through the hands, feet or main chakras; picking up of energetic information, vibrations or phenomena and the interpretation or use of vibrational stimulation and frequencies
- **Synaesthesia** – a rare and unusual mixing of the senses where one of the above triggers another; the ability to smell colour or sound, or to hear smell...

On the physical level each special sense or faculty may be thought to have a dedicated nervous system pathway. The special afferent nerves specifically related to taste and smell are the olfactory, facial, glossopharyngeal, and vagus nerves; the optic nerve is responsible for the special sense of vision while the vestibulocochlear nerve is responsible for hearing and balance.

We can see from the list above that we can take in information on the physical and also the invisible levels – we can engage the Inner Third Eye, the Chakra Third Eye, the ears, the senses of touch, taste and smell, and the nervous system messages conveyed via the existing Main Chakra system. The physical anatomy has its own meta-mirror image that corresponds to the Psychic Anatomy.

Discovering that the Psychic body connected with other energetic systems made sense. Linking and interacting with the Amygdala, the Psychic Body has third-party connection to the Earthing Chakras (particularly 5th and 8th Earthing chakras) and the Signal Chakras. We also include here the energy system housed through the Hara System to the Soul Body.

Because this is an easily recognised energetic structure working on the Soul / Spiritual level through access to

Divine Source and Earth Harmonising Energies, it will naturally register frequencies in a way not directly connected with the Senses. And the Hara Line structure echoes the central Channel of the Psychic Core.

The main focus here is a more common understanding of what is meant by the term Psychic abilities, Psychic Body or Chakras and the energy anatomy that has supported these abilities and sense-ings.

THINGS THAT CAN GO WRONG

We have had a certain amount of psychic ability and anatomy that has worked very well up until now, thank you very much – so why NOW do we have more? What is the reason for this? Why do we need to pay more attention energetically about sensory things than before?

Why indeed!

New World Problems

Things that we were never physically or energetically required to process or defend ourselves from are almost now a part of daily life.

Toxic pollution, environmental crap, technological fallout, food interference and compromise – these things are thrown at us energetically from many directions. Much of life has lost its simplicity and we tend to live very complicated lives at present. Great for variety and interest, but also quite taxing.

The Sensitive and the aware can be challenged and in the Section on "Things That Can Go Wrong" we deal with some of these current day issues; such as Chemtrails, Radionics, Prayers, Preservatives, Media Manipulations etc.

People are not sleeping as well as they used to, and it seems that there is a lot more Astral activity nowadays than ever before around Full Moon times. Many can be "open" to paranormal activity that can interrupt their sleep; and all of this can intrude on the Nervous System.

Our Crystalline Body is being challenged as never before as it attempts to hold its own frequency amidst the clamour of diverging and opposing energies in these tumultuous times.

New Era Energies

As mentioned in several of my books, we are travelling the Cosmos in a unique time, spiralling through uncharted waters, so to speak, navigating through Cosmic Winds, historic frequencies, new combinations of energies and have a chance of real Planetary Evolution.

We have come to the end of the Kali Yuga, and as such, we are in "dark times" according to some predictions. However, on a Soul level, this is one of the most interesting and exciting times in our Planetary history – this is the chance to get certain things "right" and the opportunity for many Souls to get themselves of the incarnation wheel... This includes the Planet as she battles and thrashes with those ancients reincarnated who are still hell bent on ripping out *all* of her resources before discarding her and heading for other planets and worlds to plunder.

We are in the middle of a war between Light and Dark, with the old model of duality tugging at our legs. We can sometimes see the Dark in power plays, people-control, misinformation and even self-serving by those we have entrusted; as there is Dark behind them. Likewise, there are also legions of Light working in the background, many StarSeed Angels and Earth Angels, and those willing to take stands for cruelty or ill treatments.

We seek peace because we know that that is entirely possible, just as we seek cooperation, collaboration, creativity and positivity. However, there are some Souls – I am sure we all know some of these – who do not understand these things, who are not evolved enough to *get* these concepts, and who may *never* get them – who are sentenced to complete and repay karmic debts yet who still insist on defaulting back to their own greedy, inadequate, selfish, harming ways and who are in actual fact in a process of **de**volving...!

We are then caught up in a world that contains these characters in order to really get our own individual Soul lessons on this. Painful as it is, many Sensitives are impacted with sometimes atrocious treatments and much disrespect.

Maintaining our own energy systems so that we can follow our *own* path, our *own* journey and not get caught up in the repeat dramas, tragedies and karmic backlashes of others becomes an important part of navigating our way through all of the Cosmic energies as well as the energies of others that have also been stirred up by the same.

Why New Anatomy?

So what has changed in recent years that justifies our having extra Sensory anatomy, extra Psychic Chakras?

Many things are coming to Light, are being exposed. But rather than repeat the plots and plans to gain control of our lives, our energy, our Soul even, we will leave the David Ickes of this world to portray these.

The internet is giving us a different view than that which the censored media gives us. It has been exposing things for many years, but usually most people have not been able to come to grips with the things that have been shared simply because we have often found such things hard to believe – for that is not what we would do, that is not how we would behave – and so many have chosen to ignore them and to focus instead only on those things which give them comfort, peace, hope and a feeling of safety.

However, those things are no longer working to keep the impact of the Dark at bay as before, and should we choose to continue to exist in ignorance, then our future enslavement is truly sealed. For now we are being called to live in integrity and to be clear about who we are, what we are about and how we wish OUR world to be and to function, rather than allowing others to control it for us.

The internet has been hugely instrumental in bringing hidden facts to our attention. However, this has been recognised, and is being countered. When we examine the many sources of information, we can also get lost in the disinformation fight-back by those wanting to portray any whistle-blower as a conspiracy theorist, or as a nutter. My concern here is not about the *information* fight-back, but the actual *effects* of detrimental actions that are impacting us around the world, and that Sensitives, Empaths and Psychics can be affected by and succumb too if they have no tools for clearing or understanding what is going on.

Things such as chemical inhibitions or dis-easing through Chemtrails, fluoride in water, vaccinations etc can all impact on the Sensitives ability to protect or monitor their energy systems and capabilities.

In the next Section **"What Can Affect Us"** and in the **"Tools For Working with the New Chakras"** Sections there are some ideas to combat these events.

What Can Affect Us

Anything that impacts on the Nervous System will impact on the Psychic Body!

Any energy frequency that upsets, shocks or disrupts one's neurology will affect the Sensory anatomy and the Psychic body in some way!

Rebalancing the Nervous System will not always rebalance the Psychic Chakras. So if there are neurological issues, always check the Psychic anatomy.

Some of the things that will disrupt the Nervous System and the Psychic Body are listed as follows:

- Brain Manipulation
- Chemtrails
- Media Subliminals
- Prayers
- Toxins
- Radionics
- Vaccines

Brain Manipulation: NLP

Much study has been done on the effect of language on the brain and on behaviour.

Sound is an energy wave, and many of us have discovered the power of music or poetry over mood and behaviour during our life. It is not only our ears, but also the inner brain that can be affected by sound, not just in our ability to "hear" words, but in the actual frequency that conveys such words.

The *exact* same words spoken by different people can have entirely different affect upon our sensing of what was said or of the communication therein. Even our physical body can respond similarly. As can our subtle body anatomy!

NLP - Neuro Linguistic Programming (brain and language programs and patterns) - has been around for many years now, and courses were (and probably still are) run on how to convince people to buy, how to find their key vulnerability points to make sales or to influence people. Having innocently attended a course myself to enhance my own working of the brain, when the course conversation turned to how to persuade people unethically, I decided I could not and would not utilise such tools myself, and promptly finished the course.

Many years later I came across Neuro Linguistic Kinesiology – NLK – and upon investigating further, discovered that only those tools used to enhance personal experience and to defuse blockages ethically were included in the curriculum in order to enhance the client's learning and performance abilities – and in some cases actually reversing some previous unhelpful brain programming.

As I was already a practising Kinesiologist, I found the techniques extremely helpful and so was happy to include this and even to become a qualified trainer myself.

The moral of this little story is to emphasise the importance of awareness when it comes to the tricks of others to persuade one to do things one may not normally consider. Preying on the subconsciousness of others to make a profit is actually the goal of some people, and without consideration to the purchaser this becomes unethical. "Creating a need" where there originally wasn't one is a major key to our current consumerism addiction.

Marketing can, and does, employ all the tips and tricks it can to create a market for something that they portray as necessary, to underline an inadequacy or to make one feel that they are more important than they are...etc...

You will recognise some of these tricks for yourself. Sure if you were already looking for a similar item, and the advertising gives you that bit of extra information or an added benefit and it is affordable, then it is probably harmless. But not all advertising actually sells the benefits. And so many people do not think about what is behind the advert.

Advertising is only one way of Brain manipulation. People can attempt to control one's thoughts, and there are some excellent blogs and websites on Narcissists, Sociopaths, even Psychopaths.

Politicians utilise rhetoric, well designed speeches that appeal with charismatic wordage and lofty ideals, yet often do not outline (nor would or could they ever...) the methods to achieve these things. And generally once the voting is over, the speech is dropped, the "promises" forgotten, and the pollies swim in their own money and power pig pens. Yet look at the number of people who accept and even believe their words, and who even defend their lack of action on any promised policy...

When you find the people who follow through on what they promise, who speak with honesty, then these are the people to be counted on to keep their words, and whose actual word can carry power. If they are also kind then they can be a treasure.

The words of some people can trigger pre-installed beliefs, buried fears, covert claims, suppressed emotions, dormant desires, secret entitlements... some people can do this to help heal them, others do this to gain allegiance or control – the ability to recognise these things is priceless to keep one's freedom and autonomy.

Words carry energy. In verbally transmitted energy can be hidden codes, hidden intentions. A word of kindness can be true balm, a supposedly kind word can also be threatening – recognising the energy behind the word may be vital to be free from accepting any negative, limiting or harmful code via language and the spoken word.

Some sounds or words can be viewed as "carrier" frequencies – If you saw the movie or read the book *"Contact"* by Carl Sagan, you would appreciated that there can be several levels to codes. Hidden codes can be installed via something that appears to be harmless at the time, but later is activated.

Sensitives and those on a spiritual journey who have stood up to the Dark in previous incarnations are generally the ones who will have experienced some of this, and in these times, these hidden, buried or historic codes may emerge to be dealt with. This can only lead to good if we can clear these as they emerge, for this leads to ultimate freedom, authenticity and evolution.

What you can do

Keeping our brain free from such codes, attending to clearing and rebalancing the Nervous System, our inner psychic brain centres and our outer sensory psychic anatomy can be a powerful protection against such unwanted intrusions. Check for any unwanted or harmful "recordings" or "rogue programs" in these areas and remove these also.

"I am 100% free from the projections, intents, pushy thoughts and judgements of others. I now easily recognise sales, media and marketing manipulation and I also willingly recognise faulty logic and quasi-reasoning."

"I now know what is a want and what is a need for me, and I have the right to my own opinion on these things without peer or family or partner or sales pressure."

"I am perfect and acceptable exactly as I am."

Chemtrails

Just one from the range of new toxicities we encounter in modern day life, but worthy of special mention here.

There is now an emerging recognition, especially with the release of pictures, videos and even pilot's confessions that Chemtrails (not Contrails, which some official sources attempt to claim are these noxious sky vapour trails) have been operating for many years now. There has been no real explanation given as to why this practice has continued, and continues, and the public have been kept in the dark for a long time about it.

But the results are coming in, and my understanding is that further health studies are being undertaken. Finally. Yet even these studies are totally unnecessary when one breaks down the contents of Chemtrail sprays and investigates many of the components separately...

Chemtrails containing Barium, Lithium, aluminium to name a few. Now some countries are attempting to legalise **vaccination** patents delivered by aerial spray...! And this without the consent of the population they are wanting to spray!

Chemical sprays that rain down on in certain areas can be felt by our Sensory energy apparatus. It can affect our ability to communicate with our self, and is mirrored

in our ability to navigate energetically in the world at large.

What can we do about this?

Check and clear the Crown Chakra, Shoulder Transducer Chakras, Spatial Chakras Ankle and Stability Chakras, Causal Chakra, Integumentary System and Nervous System.

Talking with and to your body, to your anatomy, to your own inner knowing and autonomy and making positive reclamation statements such as those listed here can override much of the intended or inherent damage.

Reclaim your own body right down to the cellular level, free from all external pollutants.

"My body consciousness, my psychic anatomy, my total energy systems now 100% refuse to take on board or to process any and all chemicals from Chemtrails or from related toxic release or spillage, so be it"

"I reclaim my own separate anatomy from the world at large; I resist safely, easily, elegantly any attempts to subdue me, my body, my mind and my journey, so be it."

"I now 100% reclaim my own body at the cellular level to be safely and easily 100% free from all external pollutants. I no longer accept that which would inhibit me, and I throw it off."

Media Subliminals

Media is often about sensationalising something. At one time news was simply the reporting of facts. Then fabricating stories began to be hinted at, next followed propaganda though it is never labelled as that.

Today we cannot wholly trust everything written in the paper. Even allowing for simple mistakes, the men behind the printing press, the media owners, often have their own agenda – or the agenda of someone over them...

The sharing of knowledge on the internet had educated many. It has opened up a whole new world, and things that happen all over the world can be at the click of a mouse...

Further sophistication and further deviance is now attempting to discredit the honest and open reporting of facts. Anyone can say anything, and thus we have the discrediting websites, the websites set up by people wishing to hide something and who attempt to deride and discredit all those who oppose their own stance (or profits).

We could go on about media, but this is mainly about the subliminals employed with or through media.

One of these subliminals is the use of images; via video or picture posts. Have you noticed how some movie trailers or "exciting moments" are portrayed with a series of quick mili-second pictures that we think we don't have time to register fully with the naked eye? I find them distressing as they confuse the brain (as they are intended to do) and when a series of quick snapshots starts, I avert my eyes... The disruption to our ability to concentrate is becoming obvious in some of the newer generations, and it feels like an assault on my own consciousness when this visual pummelling starts.

Some advertising can use one second long quick shots to entice and portray a message – "One picture is worth a thousand words" – but even this I find annoying, knowing what I know about the effect on assaulting the barriers in the brain. Add to this the subliminal messages, the pictures that the brain would not normally accept, and you get an installed subliminal, a message that can be totally contrary to all you want to know or to hold dear. I don't like to take any chances, as my brain is mine and I want it to stay that way.

At some level, Sensitives know when their vision has been impacted, though they may not know why or where from. I always question why the need for any series of quick images, and clear my sensory visual centres after.

Another "subliminal" is the tracking of everything that anybody keys into their computer. Harmless as it may be, advertising pays money for your shopping and internet browsing history. But for the Sensitive, the sense can be of someone looking over your shoulder…

On another darker note, governments are now gathering information via nay means available on any citizen that connects with their country. Huge databanks hold files and records of phone conversations, internet interactions, medical records, travel histories and anything else that may possibly be perceived to come under the guise of "Homeland Security" – regardless of the truth.

Google is a very helpful tool but their terms of usage also have a clause claiming total right over any intellectual property that is sent via their email or systems. Having actually read through their terms I now use a browser and search engine (Firefox and StartPage searches) that hides all of my searches from Google and I only ever use Google email for anything that doesn't matter – for Google are also setting up their own data banks of information – not that I have anything to hide, but if I wanted all of my mail to be read by a total stranger or to be kept for the next twenty years or so, then I might as well give everybody my passwords, bank info and diaries now - in short, I would actually own nothing of my own intellectual property nor have any part of my mind or my life that is clearly mine or private. I do not see that as freedom, nor as even democratic considering that I have not given permission for this to happen.

When this sort of thing happens to Sensitives, they can feel compromised or even unsafe. This should be unnecessary, but our Sensory equipment can register that it is being spied upon in some way in its attempts to protect us and keep us feeling safe and secure.

What can we do about it?

Learning how to pull one's mind, one's energy, out of interactions on the internet and learning how to release the energy of nosey others can assist here.

With our Sensory Psychic anatomy, I suggest the Spatial Chakras, Eye Chakras, Transpersonal, Navel and Crown Chakras be cleared and realigned. Also check inner Brain Centres for installation of any subliminal messages via visual or auditory means.

Being aware of these subliminals can assist in monitoring as you go, and in refusing to accept that which is not for your highest good.

The Affirmations for *Brain Manipulation* can assist here.

Prayers

The power of Positive Thinking and Thought can impact and heal. Dr Masaru Emoto studied and photographed the impact of thought on water and water crystals. His amazing findings confirmed what many spiritual and intuitive people already knew. The human body is around 80-95% water, and this can be impacted by energy, frequencies and thought. When a prayer is said many miles away and there is a remote healing that takes place, this also affirms the same concept.

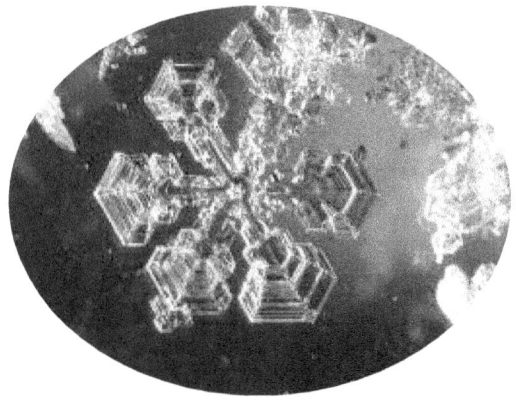

However, the same can be said for negative intention, too. People can think bad thoughts about one, or send unhealthy thoughts, and these can impact on the sensitive and the open. When people who are "praying" for something harmful to "happen" to someone to prove that their "God" is the right God, their God is the Only God, and that anything that does not comply with their views of how others should be, they can impact on energy healers, intuitive, mystics and the Sensitive. Ignorance may be the cause, but this highlights the short-fall of any religion that cannot allow others to find their own way to the Light.

"Pointing the Bone", Voodoo and other nasties may have an impact on the Sensitive or the receptive. Psychic Attack by someone deliberately intending harm can stymie one's progress.

As a Kinesiologist and vibrational energy healer I am aware of intermittent "praying" by some of my family (now ex-family) members who think that their Pentecostal religion has the right to pray that God "punishes" me and brings me to my knees for my practices because I no longer believe the same way they do. *Anybody* who talks love and peace yet prays for punishment or anything other than Love to others is certainly *not* of the Light. Many religious people are no different to anybody else yet often claim or insinuate that they are better.

It is disappointing that so many cults often default to punishment or revenge in some way rather than continue to practise that which was exhorted by their own leader, Jesus Christ, which was the message of Love.

What can we do about it?

Identify the source of any negative intent, and remove all frequencies, thoughts, messages, labels or anything that has been sent to hinder or punish from your Nervous System, Heart, Mind, Navel Chakra, Psychic Chakras and

Crystalline Body. Also check that there are no lingering belief systems on which any projections or introjections can take hold.

Reclaim your autonomy to live your life according to your own Soul's journey and destiny, in line with your own True Source. Ensure you are free from any installed "guilt" or "sinner" beliefs or codes.

Relinquish and undo any baptisms or "sealing" of energies that took place through the signing of the Cross over the Third Eye.

Reclaim your own identity and the Right to pursue your own journey.

Some suggestions:

"I am now 100% free from all allegiances, subscriptions, conscriptions, promises, vows or jurisdictions of …. (cult, belief or religious affiliation) from this point on and I commit allegiance only to my True Source and my Higher Purpose according to my Souls true intentions."

"I now 100% choose and have the right to choose my own Spiritual Journey, in alignment with my own Soul Purpose and Mission and Destiny. I 100% release safely and completely any and all judgments placed on me from any religion, "faith" or belief system that is contrary to my own. I allow my own Soul and my Higher Self to be in total charge of my journey, free from the control of others. So be it."

"I can be and am Spiritual without the need for religiosity or a man-made set of beliefs. I am now 100% ready to connect and work with my own True Divine Source according to my highest Soul journey and purpose."

Radionics

Radionics is a huge field, and its applicability related to a variety of vibrational functions in a diverse assortment of arenas. We have restricted the references here to the more common forms in order to avoid confusion.

Radionics itself was initially understood to mean a method of rebalancing that could also become a remote healing tool. The Radionics Association gives the following initial theory basis:

Basic Radionics Theory: *A method of healing at a distance through the medium of an instrument using the ESP faculty. In this way a trained and competent practitioner can discover the cause of disease within any living system, be it human being, an animal, a plant or the soil itself. Suitable therapeutic energies can then be made available to the patient to help restore optimum health. First originated by Dr Albert Abrams (1863 - 124) and further developed by others: Ruth Drown, T G Hieronymus, David Tansley etc. The basic concept is that man and all other life forms share a common ground- they are submerged in the electromagnetic field of the earth. Each life form has its own electromagnetic field and if distorted will trigger disease in that organism. All is energy.*

Initially it was used as a form of healing, using each life forms unique vibrational signature, interpreted as a system of codes or Rates. The establishing of the correct code was electronically accessed via the physical readout with a Radionics device. These could cover a wide range of organs, physiology, pathogens, poisons and toxins etc. In time, devices were built to utilise and transmit the frequencies involved both personally and remotely.

A Radionics signature could later be read from a hair, a full name, a date of birth and even a location. The correcting or corrective frequency, radio or sound wave, vibration or energy quotient was projected to infuse the *target* in order to bring about a health state again.

However...

The use of current Radionics techniques has since become corrupted in certain quarters – for some sectors now include a broadcasting of certain frequencies to confuse health rather than to support health, and this has been applied to groups, areas and cultures. Further negative sophistications can target a range of individuals of a certain type, or a certain age, or a certain consciousness... Current dark practices can include energy broadcasts to dull the mind, transmit viruses to create pandemics, maximise pharmaceutical sales, and impede the conscious and aware.

Indeed, I have felt these Radionics in the UK and in Australia for myself. I first heard of this form of energy application when a Psychic Intuitive refused to have her picture taken for the promotion of her book and an upcoming movie I was involved in making with her in the 1990's. When pressed she allowed a picture of herself side on, but refused to look directly into the camera. When I pressed her for her reasons she explained that the energy and essence of the eyes can be impacted (and "robbed") if photographed and connected with the use of Radionics. She had apparently had previous experience of this interference. Though I have not yet let this prevent me from having photos taken by those I trust, I got what she meant. She had come up against it before and did not want to "be tracked" or drained energetically in this way.

Since then there have been occasions when I have been in excellent health and have suddenly deflated energetically, showing all of the symptoms of flu or some other virus.

When tracking things to see if my Immune System had been compromised or if I had "caught" something off someone, I was surprised to discover that I had been subjected to a pharmaceutical broadcast of a virus, and hadn't actually contracted the disease. Rather the energy vibrations had been emitted on a certain geographic location (I have experienced this on occasion when in Canberra, Melbourne and Sydney) and suddenly the population is fighting off this health invader. The normal mindset being; "if I have the symptoms of the flu, then I must have the flu…"

What to do

My recognition of the frequency broadcast allowed me to refuse to take this frequency on board and enabled me to release the energy back to its source. Then to clean up any collateral damage that the frequency had triggered.

Radionics broadcasts can be picked up by our Sensory Chakras as well as our hair and skin. We can do a Mindful release of any energies or frequencies from these places.

Firstly, ensure that your Core is balanced and energised (Psychic CORE Exercise). Check and clear the Psychic Control Centres in the brain and body, and rebalance the neurology, then we address the electromagnetics and redefine these so as to be unique to one's self again.

As there can sometimes be some collateral of harm before we recognise the negative source of our discomfort, we can support the body and nervous system with care and good nutrition.

Some helpful statements:

"My Psychic centres and anatomy, my total body consciousness, my Immune System, my brain and my mind now 100% refuse acceptance of any frequencies, broadcasts, Radionics or energy projections encoded with or carrying virus frequencies, virus codes or settings. I release totally any and all absorbed related frequencies and codes and I 100% reset back to who I truly am and to my full health again."

"Any and all toxic vibrations, energy waves or frequencies broadcast or emitted from any source that is not for my highest good and best health are now released and returned to its source, never to return to me again. So be it."

"I 100% refuse to accept any alien or harmful frequencies, any harmful virus or energetic vibrations calibrated to cause dys-function or dis-ability and I reclaim my right to nurture my own body safely again. My hair, my skin and my eyes are now conduits of Light again and all dark or dirty is released completely, safely, and immediately."

Toxins

When one drives an old model truck or car, and the engine is built to handle rough or crude fuels, things can work well, and practically anything can be put into the fuel tank and the vehicle will perform. In fact, high quality fuels may even be a waste of money. Conversely, put rough or crude fuels into the latest state of the art fuel injection supercars, and things will just jam up. However, supply it with good quality clean fuel, and you will have excellent performance and a dream ride.

It is the same with our own physical vehicle. Some bodies can handle any old thing, so to speak, with little or even sometimes no really harmful consequences – depending on the constitution and genetic makeup. But some of us are more refined, and our physical (and the interplay with our energetic and sensory subtle anatomy) just can't cope with some things.

The additions in current times of substances and pollutants that didn't even exist a hundred or even fifty years ago can gravely impact the Sensitive and the refined system.

These can include:

- Fluoride
- Preservatives
- Herbicides
- Pesticides
- Additives & Food Bleaching
- Fuel Emissions
- New Plastics and Synthetic Products
- Genetically Modified Products
- Electronic Pollution and Impact

I recently saw a video using a split-open fluoride toothpaste tube placed in an attic to kill all of the mice and rats there! Not a drop left and after 3 months the rats began to return, so up into the attic went another tube of toothpaste. What does that tell you about it? And it even had instructions on the tube: "Do not swallow".... The human system usually takes some time to adapt or to build up tolerance to new or introduced foodstuffs and environmental surroundings, yet today with the introduction of so many newly developed materials and food additives our systems are being challenged to handle and multi-process these as never before.

Effects can be indicated through our skin. Sleep patterns can be affected as the body attempts to process and to "right" itself during our rest periods. The Nervous System can feel agitated and the Digestive System can be compromised, the Lymphatic System can be sluggish, and the Integumentary System (skin) can be dragged into the bodies detoxification attempts.

What can we do?

Avoid fluoride toothpaste and water as fluoride contributes to Pineal Gland calcification.

Attempting to simplify life and technology is a good beginning. Reducing preservatives etc and eating as organically as possible is another important health factor. Alkaline water may assist, Chlorella can help draw out impurities and heavy metals, Essential Oils can help support and rebalance the Nervous System.

Keeping our hair clean from chemicals as much as is possible assists them to act as the energetic antennae that they are.

Becoming aware of the "dumbing-down" effects imposed on us from a variety of sources is not about being fearful of these sources, but rather the outwitting of them and the determination to hold onto our own true nature.

Recognising the detrimental effects equips us to keep our sensory systems clear. Knowing about how to attend to any affected Sensory Chakra gives us back power and control in our own lives again.

Energy Healing, Kinesiology, Touch-For-Health, these can also aid to restore correct function again. Particularly when applied to the Nervous, Digestive, Integumentary and Lymphatic Systems.

Psychic Chakras to consider may be: Stability Chakra (Mid-Shins), Thymus, Navel, Crown Chakras – as well as the Earthing Chakras (particularly Earthing 1, 2 and 3).

Vaccines

There was a time when vaccinations helped to stop severe disease from spreading throughout whole communities. There was a collaboration to destroy that which might destroy humanity. Or animals.

We have come a long way since then. Improved hygiene and cleanliness has protected us from common and dangerous pathogens and bacteria such as salmonella, botulism, and other sundry skin or stomach infectors. We have almost swung the other way by banishing healthy bacteria that contribute to a stronger Immune System. However, the reduction of disease is not all caused by vaccinations, though this has certainly helped.

The current vaccinations schedules seem to have taken a life and a reign of control all of their own; instead of the few vaccinations that were manageable by tiny infants and children in the 50's to 80's we have seen a terrifying increase in the total number of multi-vaccinations that has impacted the young and has raised the number of autistic cases per thousand through the roof.

No doctor or nurse dare yet give a guarantee that there is *nothing harmful* in their vaccinations. Indeed, the ingredients now reads more like a list of prohibited poisons, so much so that each vaccination phial has in its little box an instruction and warning leaflet as to its contents (never questioned by supposedly knowledgeable medics) and its possible side effects, even listing "death"... In America, there have been documented cases of over thirty deaths in the last 5 years alone, of doctors who have spoken up and researched about the harmful impacts of current multi-vaccinations. I give very conservative figures here...

The push to compulsive vaccination goes against our human rights to choose for our self, and the argument that we should all be vaccinated does not answer the basic question; "If you're afraid of me because I am unvaccinated, does that mean your vaccines don't work?"

What has this to do with our sensory anatomy? Well, there are two things.

One is that all vaccinations are designed to penetrate the blood-brain-barrier (BBB) to deliver the virus / disease / bacteria straight into the central neurology and brain fluids - and subsequently into the body tissues anything that is carried in these bombarding fluids.

In effect, they override the Immune System, infect the body and transport poisons directly into the brain.

Toxic detergents in these vaccinations destroy the BBB, allowing more toxins to enter the brain, which can lead to programmed cell death and disease. Permanent altering of brain function can be caused by unwanted toxins entering the brain, all because of a destroyed brain barrier system. Too early vaccination, over vaccination, multiple vaccinations all tend to deliver the opposite of what is claimed – health. Dependency on chemical medication and a lifelong sentence to support pharmaceutical companies and their healthy profits is guaranteed. The only things that get healthy through vaccinations nowadays are the wallets of the PharmaCos.

Two. The other issue is that compulsory vaccinations sets the stage for enforced wholesale interjection of any foreign substance that the governing bodies see fit to legislate. Just think about that... It gives others the rights and the power to put into *your* body, and your *children's* bodies, **anything** that they have a legal permit to inject into it! And legal permits are bought. Patents are applied for and paid for. Even for aerial vaccinations! And having the substance that the governing body insists on infecting everyone with is a money-printing machine... whose profits can be stored elsewhere... and there is no, I repeat NO, responsibility for guaranteeing the safety of any of the products.

What can you do?

Once damage is done to the Nervous and Immune Systems, it takes a long time and a long fight to regain health again. Herbal medicine and acupuncture can assist to support the body, and nature, nurture and positive thought can assist. Retraining the brain and neurology once damage has been repaired can help.

But the most powerful tool is prevention!

On an energetic level, removing any codings carried in via these vaxxes can allow quicker recovery, if there is the possibility of such. Clear any infected organs and their relevant Chakras and support these vibrationally (colour, Essential Oils, herbs, nutrition etc). Clearing shock and trauma from the Nervous System and on a cellular level will assist the body to hold the incremental healings as you go. (The New Signal Survival Chakras can also greatly assist with correcting in-body energetic connection and communication here – see *"The New Evolved Chakras"* book.)

On the Psychic Chakras level, you may find the psychic centres in the brain will have distortions through vaxxes, and will require regular clearings and healings as well as monitoring.

Clear the Light Channels in the head, clear and clean all filters encountered, and remove all psychic phlegm and plasma with Essential oils where indicated.

Key points to look at are the back of the head at the Occipital – The Psychic Gateway, as well as its opposing Chakra at the front of the forebrain; the Transpersonal, and all interlinking psychic brain centres.

Heavy Metal toxicity can be assisted with high quality **Chlorella**, which attracts and attaches these molecules and escorts them out of the tissues, bloodstream and body. This helps to clear the brain and contributes to repair of the BBB.

SENSORY PSYCHIC ANATOMY DETAILS

INCLUDES:

PSYCHIC ANATOMY

IN-BODY, OUT-OF-BODY CHAKRAS

HEAD CHAKRAS

BODY CHAKRAS

PSYCHIC CONTROL CENTRES

ACCESS POINTS & POSITIONS

MASTER GATEWAY CHAKRAS

PSYCHIC CHAKRAS; HEAD ANATOMY

So just what are the Psychic Head Chakras if not just the Crown Chakra, the Third Eye and the in-head Chakras discovered by the Vedics?

We will attempt to approach these from the head down.

Looking first at the Psychic Chakras connected with this extra-ordinary system of perception that have Access / Contact Points that are external to the Head we have quite a collection in the head area.

Viewing them clairvoyantly or psychically or scanning them etherically external to the body we will discover these amazing outer Chakra points.

Having learned of the Transpersonal Chakra many years ago, I was already aware of the "Unicorn" effect of this Chakra. I then discovered that it worked with the Psychic Chakras and was also part of that system. We will come back to this in a moment.

Then I discovered something new and unexpected to me.

Two etheric antennae that look like "horns" appear to emerge from the frontal lobes either side of the hairline.

I was amazed when I first felt these on a very psychic person who made her living helping others but who was suffering a great deal of pain herself.

On further examination it was clear that one of these antennae was actually stuck or glued in place at a distance of approximately 8" (20cms) external to the body; it had been caused through picking up too much negative gunk from others. And this had caused it to be stuck in a continually "On" mode, and though weak was always attempting to function – a bit like having a foot on the starting motor. The other Chakra was still able to retract, but had been compromised functionality-wise by the malfunction of the other.

Many people do not have this problem as their "horns" are poorly developed so they may remain constricted within the head, like the nubs of antlers on a young deer. But those who have been using their antennae – whether knowingly or not – run the risk of picking up everything in the atmosphere, both energetic and emotional. Learning how to care for and retract this important energetic anatomy can be important for the survival of some Sensitives.

The Integumentary System (Skin) and Hair must also be included as part of the Psychic Body. Hair acts as antennae, and there may well be times when the hairs on our arms have stood up on end having picked up some energetic occurrence. The skin can goose-bump up as well.

This usually happens when this system picks up the Astral, Paranormal or Etheric energy of someone or something close by and can serve as a *warning* or a *confirmation*.

The Antennae, Psychic Horns, Horn Antennae

There are several names for this particular anatomy, as they are all descriptive of their function.

As you can see there is an energetic protrusion on each side of the Frontal Lobes extending up and out in a similar manner to "horns" and these are approximately positioned just inside the hair line or scalp.

A famous picture of *Moses* by Jose De Ribera shows his Psychic Antennae or "Rays of Light" as they are claimed to be called – they can be seen quite clearly and he has *never* been called demonic. Not that I am aware of anyway. In ancient times, these same "Horns" were included in pictures and sculptures, demonstrating not a demonic or devilish image, but the image of a wise sage. His statue by Michelangelo in the Library of Congress also shows these two protrusions from his head.

They are an interpretation of the "horn like rays" emitted from Moses at these points. And this is precisely what the antennae are in highly developed psychics.

Their function is to act as receivers of energetic information, picking up frequencies, and channelling these incoming frequencies into the brain centres and inner Psychic Chakras for interpretation and action.

Many people are now not only growing these but also developing them further. I have noticed these in a lot of my clients though they were not always present in everyone when I first started working with these Chakras some time ago.

Main problems usually occur when they appear to be kind of "rusting"-in-place – especially with psychics who have never closed them down, or turned them off. Or they have become badly gunked or gummed and stuck in sensitive types who have not fully recognised their abilities but been prone to input overwhelm or attack from others.

One psychic I know went a bit mental because she never, ever closed them down or retracted them in. Her energetic information systems were continually on alert, always picking up information, and these ever changing vibrations were, in part, running her life.

She was so set to be "tuned-in" that she also had the habit of interfering with people she had (nosily) picked up information about, whether it was her business or not. This is not only unethical but also unhealthy. Besides which, no one should be subjected to a psychic approaching them uninvited with whatever story interpretation they have and that they wish to impress upon them. It is none of their business really.

Particularly if one is going through a series of energetic or personal changes, and is part way through a "story" or chapter in their healing process then a psychic snapshot of issues by any casual psychic observation can be totally way off, for they have not been a party to the progression to this point, nor has the client yet reached the end point of this integration. What is actually a releasing and a resolving of a symptom may be erroneously interpreted as an actual issue on its own – and consequently handled incorrectly. Often an old story or issue has to emerge energetically to be fully released, not simply subdued back down again…

When this person interfered with my own clients, I had to put a stop to it, and rather than her recognising that she may have been a bit off-beam about things, she became very dark and nasty. Her own antennae were so overwhelmed with information that she was not always correct anyway in her interpretations, and she was psychically exhausted by all of the psychic activity and information.

If she learned to retract her horns antennae regularly, and to give her senses a chance to rest and rebalance and clear, she would have been less energetically excitable and over-reactive. Other clients of mine have been taught this and were so relieved to be able to find the rest they needed from continually attempting to "be on alert" and to "be ready to read" the energies.

This continual psychic alertness is not necessary and is possibly self destructive. Choose your times, choose your places.

These Chakras **can** be cleaned up and retracted back into the skull again, and re-educated to perform retraction when they are not required.

To do so, they need to be "oiled" or to have the "rust" or "gunk" removed which has jamming them into a partially or fully "On" position. Gentle manipulation by the practitioner can un-jam these, as the Etheric frequencies from the indicated Essential Oil (on a tissue) can also assist in both cleaning and oiling. Gently and very carefully working these antennae Chakras in extension and contraction can allow them to remember their options and functions.

Access / Contact Point

The Horn Contact Points are located approximately 12 – 20 cms (5 – 8 inches) out above the temples at an angle similar to a pair of horns. If one cannot feel their presence until they are found close to or on the skull, then it is usually because that they have either not been activated, cannot be activated or have been retracted at some point and have remained there through being "glued" in place with psychic gunk or somesuch.

A careful and gentle "drawing"-them-up action will indicate any serious resistance, as will a careful and gentle push down motion. When they gently respond and you (or your client if you are working on them) feel easier about these, then they are clear. Test to see what

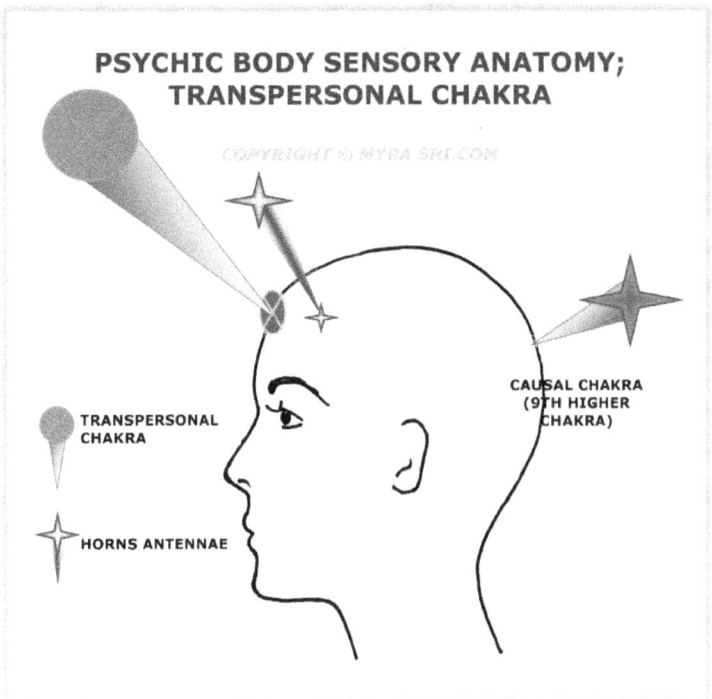

it feels like to consciously withdraw and extend them.

Transpersonal Chakra

The Transpersonal Chakra is sometimes known as the **Frontal Chakra.** The functions of the Transpersonal Chakra interact with and affect the Pineal Gland, the Temporal lobes in the Brain, and associated Psychic Brain Centres. This Chakra and the frontal brain lobes are involved with not only **direct** communication, but also with its interpretation. They filter information and dialogue then instigate the results and input back to other physiological aspects, affecting physical and emotional output and behaviour. Differences in each other's perceptions can be registered here, which can contribute to the resulting dialogue.

Avoidance in direct communication willingly or otherwise can result in a Transpersonal Chakra that is bent or leaning downward or to one side, often the result of trauma, depression, danger or direct attack or bullying from a more forceful mind. As its name implies, it is about one's persona as well as one's personal views.

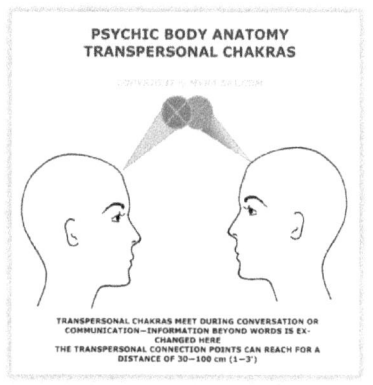

Very strong views or mind intents can be transferred or can be communicated to others via this Chakra. It can become contaminated or create cross-contamination. Transferring implies the putting upon another whether appropriate or not, whilst communication implies the ability to both give and receive information and views. Cross contamination is the picking-up of someone else's stuff; being personally infected with it and also possibly passing it on to another,.

Someone who has been continually controlled or antagonised may well find it hard to accept another viewpoint from someone else other than their previous "controller". Particularly if the person that has affected their Transpersonal has a strong mind and is psychically forceful and lacking in integrity.

Access / Contact Point

The Chakra emerges from the psychic centres in the brain to protrude out at about a 45 degree angle diagonally at the hairline, appearing like a Unicorn horn. Usually it is about 30 to 50 centimetres in length, and governs direct communication with others. It often overlaps or connects with others when close to them or in communication with them, usually easily reaching 30 – 100cms to engage.

Thus non-verbal communication takes place here.

Causal Chakra

This Chakra is related to the Higher Chakras as well as the Sensory Psychic Chakras, and interfaces with the Psychic Centres in the head (Guru especially) and the Eyes. It can also relate to the Sinuses and sometimes with the Bindu Point at the back of the head. The Causal Chakra is often referred to as the 9th Higher Chakra, as it is one of the new spiritually evolved Chakras to have emerged over the last 30 years. It is also related to *indirect* communications. It also connects with the sinuses behind the eyes and with inner vision.

The contact point for this Chakra is out from the back of the head about 15-20cms, usually in a kind of line that may relate passing through the inner centres and Pituitary Gland in the brain and out to the Third Eye. Inspiration can be accessed via the Causal, as well as the reception of data and spiritual messages.

It can also be connected with the Light Channel sitting on the same height or level if you have a two-step one – to see which channel you have, see the Section on "Clear the Light Channels".

Third Eye Chakras

Most people usually think of only one Third Eye Chakra placed approximately between the eyebrows and part of the Main Chakra System. When open and working it is able to function whilst the eyes are open (or closed), providing visual information on Auras, frequencies and in some cases beings, the paranormal or entities not normally visible to the naked eye.

There is also *another* psychic eye and this is the Inner Eye. This is placed slightly lower down, close to mid-eyebrows or even the bridge of the nose and is available when the eyes are *closed*. It allows us to access information from within our own head where we can visualise and view from there. The data accessed is via our mind and intellect but not on a thinking-functionality level, more on an "impression-reception" level.

Importantly it can also provide us with a clear space or inner screen on which to see external frequencies that our normal vision cannot access. As Neo in "The Matrix" with his blindfold on did, when we clear and train this area we may well be able to see things normally unavailable to us. Both of these psychic "Third Eyes" interact with the Pineal Gland and the Ajna Chakra, and can also connect to the Guru Chakra and the Transpersonal Chakra (illustrations to follow later).

Access / Contact Point
Approximately 5 cm or 2" from the mid-brow area.

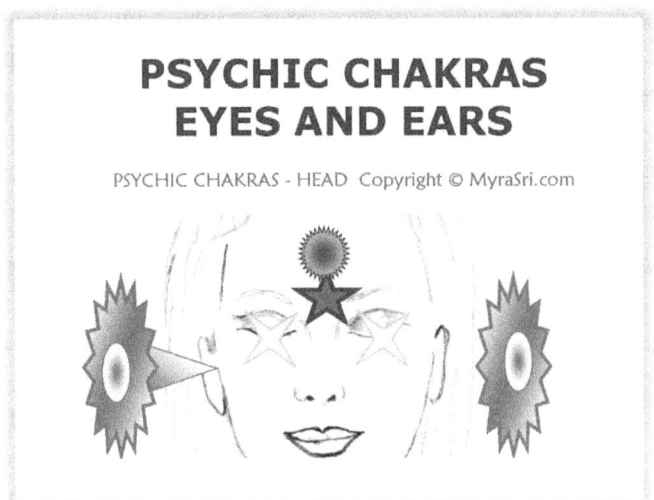

Eye Chakras

Not only do we have Third Eye Chakras, but we also have energy receptors linked to the Psychic Body in the *eyes*. Energetic information is passed from one person's eye to another's eye; a stronger force may override the current state or autonomy of a weaker force – Will Power channelled through the eyes is very real. Fortunately, when we are attuned with our eye Chakras, we can withstand this energetic assault via the optic nerves, though we may remember the encounter for some time. The follow-up *secret* being to ensure that no dumpings or codings were passed along the energetic line at the time – or remain somewhere in the energy systems. Meeting up with a really dark Soul can imprint and affect via the eyes until all taint or resonance from such beings has been cleared out of **all** Chakras and energy bodies.

The Eye Chakras include the external access points and pass information along an energy line right through to the back of the retina, where it interfaces with the optic nerve. This interfaces with the internal psychic centres, brain and the nervous system.

The real origin of both Eye Chakras are actually inside the head where the optical nerves meet to cross-over and loop at the back of the brain, sitting in the place of interpretation of incoming information. The Connection Points external to the eyes serve to contact this entire energetic optical system.

These Chakras can become clouded by another person attempting to occupy or "See" into someone's mind, or to "See" through their eyes. The clouding can cause us to blink often or to feel like we have a film across our eyes. Caused by psychic gunk or dis-resonance from the other's visioning, this can prevent easy vision. The eyes can also cloud up like this when we attempt to see into a situation that is not appropriate for us to "read" at this time, or that has harmful, negative, incompatible or toxic frequencies to one's own.

The simplest method to clear is to wipe the external Chakra point itself with a (selected) Essential Oil on a tissue, taking care not to touch the eyes or the eyelids. Wipe in front of the eyes and also at the back of the head at a similar distance. One can draw the Essential Oil energetically into the visual areas by imagination, my breathe technique (in *Secrets Beyond Aromatherapy*) or by intention, in order to clean and clear along the entire optical nerve system. Dispose of any used tissues safely and hygienically as the tissue will have gathered toxic or negative etheric phlegm or psychic plasma.

Access / Contact Point
Approximately 4-7 cm (1 ½" to 3") external to the closed eye.

Eyes & Eye Hooks

There was an exercise encouraged in some arenas that required sitting with another person in silence and just gaze (or look) into their eyes for some period of time. It was publicized as a "healing" process and one which would break down barriers. And some people who had been estranged from each other actually found a deep emotional connection once again. But these already knew the people involved. To practise this with total strangers moves things into quite a different area.

This exercise may (or may not) be safe for some people to do, but we would caution the Sensitive to guard the eyes as access points to their inner being.

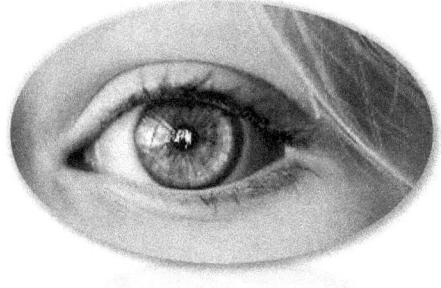

"The eyes are (indeed) *the windows of the Soul"* and also the eyes can be the windows to the Soul, if another is searching for a connection or for control. This kind of self exposure to someone incompatible, inappropriate, with mental or emotional problems or someone who is an energy taker can cause no end of trouble. If left unacknowledged or untreated, energy transfer this way can cause discomfort in the eyes *and* in the mind of the recipient. People can also try to look through your eyes, in order to "see" how *you* see the world, or what you

yourself see in a given situation. This can cause eye irritation in Sensitives.

I believe that looking into the eyes of your lover, your child, a friend or family member whom you love or trust can be a wonderful experience.

Bridges can be crossed, heart to heart understandings exchanged, and spiritual connection enhanced.

But this specific eye-gazing exercise is not necessarily suitable or healthy for eye contact with just anybody or with strangers. Who knows what lurks behind the eyes of some people...?

Whilst in this section we would like to mention an interesting phenomena regarding eyes and eye contact. This only seems to affect certain people, but in my experience, they have all been Sensitives.

Energetic connections can be made via our Chakras to those we have a close contact or intimate connection with (i.e. Heart to Heart). This connecting can take the form of a kind of energy thread or cord, like a finger of floating light that energetically attaches from one to the other, and often each to the other in return. These generally disengage until the next time - unless there is a really deep connection.

Not all connections are based on mutual love, care or consideration. Whilst there may not be deliberate intention to be harmful, they can create an energy bridge that allows a form of bleed-through of one person's energy issues or emotions. In the worst case scenario, they can impact as a Control energy, even having a form of hook on the end. This can be to any Chakra but through the eyes it has connections straight to the Psychic Body and the Heart.

Energy cords with hooks have intention to have some level of control behind them. This **"Eye Hook"** is what Leonie A David (Medical Intuitive) has discovered. Usually it is the right eye, and may be accompanied by feeling imbalanced, depressed, have itchy or sensitive eyes, redness, constant blinking, or even a stinging all of which I have experienced myself. Eye drops or ointment does not fix this! These *Right Eye Hooks* can go to the Third Eye, and can be karmically connected – there may have been some form of psychic control in a past life. This experience or memory of when one was psychically controlled in the past may leave one open to being hooked again in present day.

This kind of hook can impede one's normal systems and override the Nervous System, and a variety of other things, depending on the hook and its source. If the "hook-er" has any Dark energy within, this will certainly affect the recipient.

Feel free to contact myself or Leonie as these energy hooks through the right eyes can be very challenging for the inexperienced or unknowledgeable healer to deal with. There are many variables related to this issue and we are very familiar with this occurrence and understand the causes. The causes are generally necessary for a full clearing.

Ear Chakras

The Inner point for the Ear Chakra is about 2-5 cm internal and the Outer Ear Chakra position is approximately 5-15 cm (2"-6") external to the body.

The Ears generally function and collaborate with other Psychic head Chakras, in particular the Transpersonal, the Horn Antennae, Third Eye and the Cerebral Psychic Chakras in the Brain. Interestingly they operate separately to the Eye Chakras, though they may well collate their incoming information within the Master Centres in the Brain through the Psychic Centres.

Access / Contact Point

The Outer Ear Chakra position is approximately 5-15 cm horizontally external to the body. An Essential oil at this point, or an energetic clearing can begin the clearing process.

Ear Filters

The ears often have protective filters and these need to be cleaned occasionally or as needed. These filters serve to protect and filter out toxic or angry words, but over time can become filthy and cease to function properly.

Enlisting and instructing the client to clean their own filters energetically empowers them. The use of colour to clean and strengthen in the following sequence is considered very helpful:

- Locate the filters inside the ears, one at a time
- Gentle removal of filters; bathe to clean off all gunk in etheric soapy water
- Rinse and repair in one of the indicated: turquoise / aqua marine / light aqua / or spectrum blue-aqua

- If you are able, follow with a rinse and infusion of one of the following colour frequencies as indicated: gold / turquoise / royal blue / silver / platinum
- Before replacing, ask your client to clean behind and inside the inner ear with choice of: soap, shower, spray, any colour or method they choose
- Gently replace filter
- Recheck ear Chakras and filters after clearing
- Recheck tone of the Psychic Body anatomy again for confirmation of positive change
- Always dispose of all cleaning waters and receptacles as you go

This can make a huge difference to one's sense of well-being. And ability to really hear energetic nuances in conversation again.

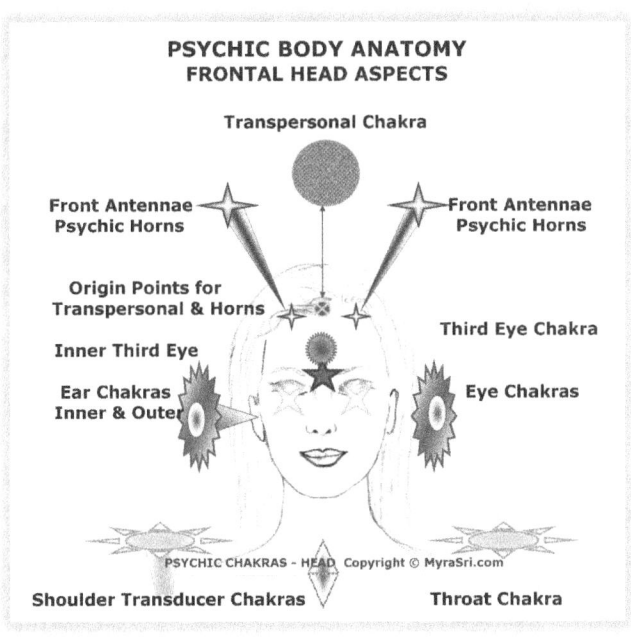

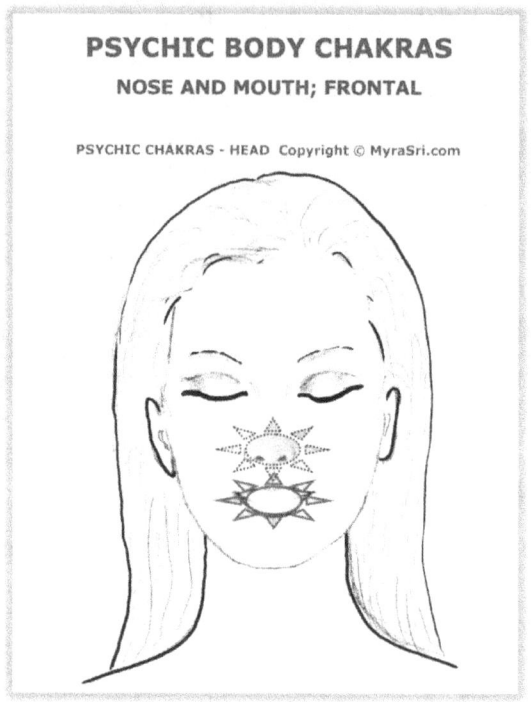

Nose and Mouth Chakras

These Chakras are actually upgraded rather than newly evolved, for these have been present and functioning in most people for some time. With the inflow of the new energies though, some may find that these senses are either more enhanced or more inhibited when they assess them.

Nose Chakra

Connected to one's Inner Knowing in the ordinary person the Nasal Chakra is often undeveloped or covered with psychic phlegm or gunk. Coughs and continual colds may indicate some sort of energetic overlay from another who is more energetically or psychically stronger or an incompatible person. Or someone who "gets up your nose". A "cold" is not necessarily always because of a virus.

It may also or alternatively indicate a tight restriction on trusting what one knows (nose), or it may be connected with a lack of self-trust. As humans, many of us have learned "to comply" in order to maintain harmony or safety, which has meant a quarantine on following our own knowing; until we mature or we learn differently!

Access / Contact Point
Best location is approximately 5cms (2") from the nose.

Mouth Chakra

This Psychic Chakra is the only one besides the Eyes that engages with giving out as well as receiving information. It actually starts at the back of the tongue, though the Chakra range is about 3 inches or 10 cms external to the mouth and can be accessed at this point.

It is capable of harnessing inner power and psychic abilities, bringing healing or condemnation (depending on the spiritual development of the being) to the recipient.

It may be influenced by the Amygdala unless this becomes more evolved.

Access / Contact Point
Contact Point is best located about 5-10cms from the mouth.

Throat Chakra

The Throat Chakra in the Psychic Body system governs self expression, one's own truth and the holding back of words and thoughts. It is usually not considered as part of the Psychic Body, but its power with language, truth and prophesying must not be underestimated. Because of its connection with the Mouth Chakra it has been included as part of the Psychic Body anatomy. It may be affected by intent to control what one says by another, or where there is conflict regarding what one says being heard.

Access / Contact Point

Anywhere along a trajectory ending approximately 3-15cms from the body.

Shoulder Transducers Chakras

These particular Chakras located above the shoulders are Master Gateway Chakras and are covered in the *Master Gateway Chakras* Section.

The Highly Sensitives Guide to Sensory Psychic Chakras

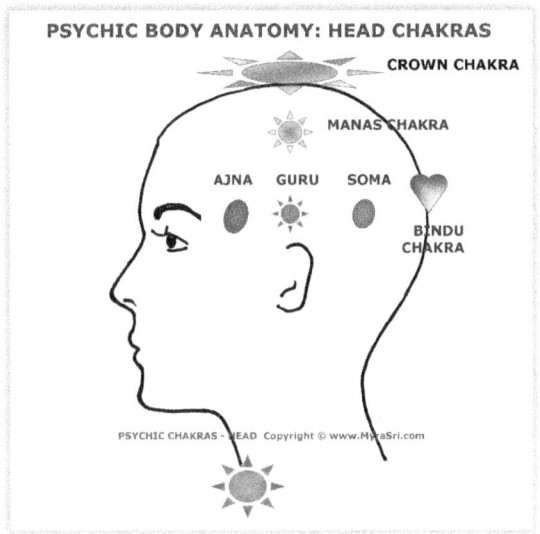

PSYCHIC HEAD CHAKRAS

Let us explore the head anatomy and Psychic Centres IN the brain... This illustration indicates the positions of possible present or active Chakras in the head.

Not everybody may have these, and indeed not everyone may *need* these, though most people will have one or more in some form or another, even if it is only a partly operative Ajna, which is closely equated to the Third Eye and the Pineal Gland. (The names indicated are from the Vedic system which has been around for centuries.)

The associated cerebral centres in the brain that work with the Psychic Chakras and related psychic senses are considered to be Master Psychic Centres. They are roughly located in the Lateral Ventricle in the Brain. Here there is a lot of fluid, and it provides a conducive and conductive energy sphere for energetic information, electrical and nerve or neuro-transmitter processing.

Fluid itself is highly conducive to lightning-fast communication and aids the ease of sharing impressions, vibrations and consciousness.

Areas in the brain involved with actual thinking link in with psychic data and impressions to create a sense perception, picture or internal image for interpretation. These thinking centres may be evolution-dictated (often through the family line) but an expanded consciousness and a higher Soul purpose can override an inhibited genetic awareness and also further enhance function, usually in a spiritual way rather than a psychic-egoic way. Major family or social restrictions can also serve to inhibit function, though with a higher calibre Soul the being may well eventually overcome some of any resultant debility.

Interactions on the physical level are with the Pituitary (via the Crown), the Hypothalamus, the Amygdala and on a psychic level with the Pineal via the Third Eye and other related centres in the Brain.

Psychic Centres; The Brain

Some of our original sensory anatomy may have remained unchanged for centuries, however, there have been upgrades and changes, and I present my current understandings here of the inner centres within the head that govern or relate to psychic function.

The Crown Chakra is an essential element in the Main Chakra system. It is also an important Psychic Chakra. As such it receives spiritual information on one level, and it also communicates etherically on another level.

The Crown (Sahasrara) Chakra is a comprehensive Chakra and emerges above the head. It also sits in the Crown of the head itself and the underside faces downward directly over the **Manas** and **Guru** Chakras, interacting directly with them.

The Crown Access or Contact Point can be reached directly on the head and up to approximately 4-12 cms above it.

The information through and from the Crown Chakra is related to one's own personal understanding, and this impacts on the interpretations of the sensory and energetic information and impressions received. Its Psychic function is through its ability to interact with the **Manas** and **Guru** Chakras below it.

As the **Manas** and **Guru** Chakras are energetically related directly to the Crown Chakra, information from the Crown merges into the Manas with the Guru facing upward.

Another main energy component is the **Pituitary Gland** which governs hormonal output and regulation. Imbalance here may affect sensory perception or interpretation as it may cause interference regarding "mood". It is usually related to the **Guru Chakra** and interacts with it.

The gland associated with the **Third Eye** is the **Pineal Gland** and both are associated with the **Ajna Chakra**. This generally emerges from the near the centre of the brain through the front of the forehead and out between the eyebrows, showing itself as the **Third Eye Chakra**. The **Ajna** is also energetically related to the Amygdala.

The **Soma** is energetically related to the Bindu Chakra which sits on the back of the head.

The **Bindu** Chakra is located at rear of head, which some refer to as the **Download Point.** However, the Bindu can also connect with the Causal Chakra in certain instances; though the **Causal Chakra** (9th Higher Chakra) is separate they may interface. The **Causal Chakra** sits external and angled up somewhat from the Bindu at the back of the head though this relationship seems to have shifted recently as illustrated in the **Psychic Control Centres** Section.

The Causal Chakra tends to receive more cosmic or spiritual data and information than the Bindu, and the Causal tends to show only in those who are on a spiritual path or mission or who have worked on themselves energetically and spiritually.

Note:

"**Gu**" means darkness and "**ru**" means light. Guru is the light that dispels the darkness of ignorance.

The **Bindu** Chakra lies beneath the cowlick that most people have at the **back of their head.** Anatomically it is located at the sutures where the bones of the back and sides of the skull meet (the occiput and the parietal). The Bindu point can feel like a tickling sensation when activated.

Keeping one's own Mind and Psychic Centres free and clear of others' and from others is important for optimal function.

The Highly Sensitives Guide to Sensory Psychic Chakras

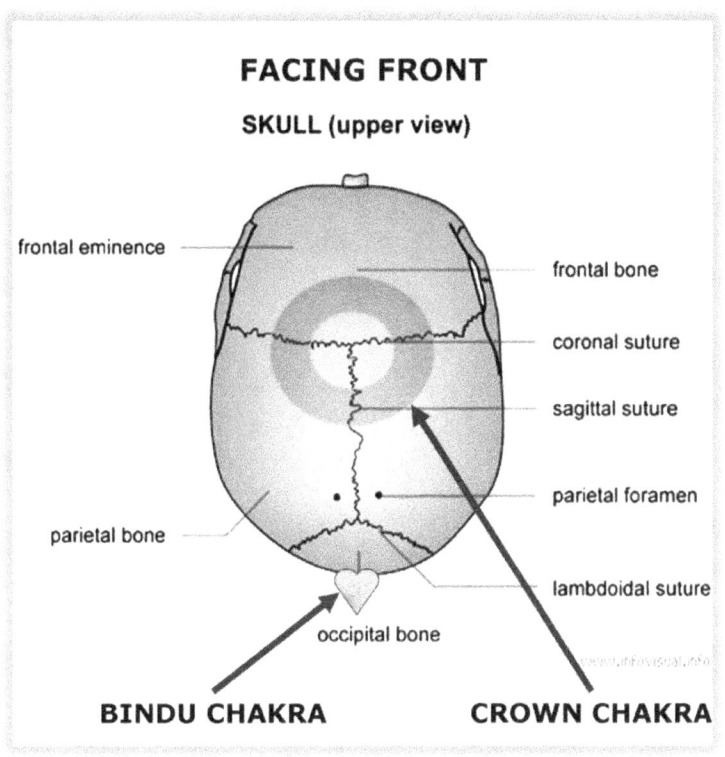

PSYCHIC GATEWAY

Where the Occiput bone meets the Atlas at the top of the spine, there is a major psychic centre.

This vital point has sometimes been used as an "escape" hatch by one or more of the energy bodies, the Soul itself or part of one's spirit; this escaping usually having occurred due to some trauma, horror or terror early in childhood, in the womb, or around conception. It is usually accompanied by a desire to leave the body and escape to a happier or safer place, usually back to one's Soul Home. See *"Case Histories"*.

If the client has escaped this way in the past, there may be a weakening in this area or an established tendency to use this point when highly stressed and this too may need addressing. This may also cause it to be susceptible to negative attack.

There may be some clouding with this area which may be hidden if of historic origin, so if there is a need to work with it, approach it gently and be mindful to send love and safety to gain correct access and for permission to attend to this sensitive spot.

TIP: When used as an escape hatch by the Soul I would suggest the following: Seal by closing down the Gateway Chakra here, seal with Circle of Light and Cross (X or +) of Matter. If possible and if you are capable, ask the client's Soul to undertake not to habitually do this again (check for a genuine agreement). Heal any old Trauma wherever it lies on whatever level, dimension, lifetime or body. Affirm that this Gateway is available for important information, but not for habitual escape, or easy access or invasion by others. Check both Front and Back Points for correct "In" / "Out" energy settings and finally re-establish harmony with other Gateway Chakras (Spatial Chakras).

Access / Contact Point

Contact may be directly via the skin (preferably with the client holding their own head there, but the **best** and cleanest facilitating contact position may well be 8-15cms away from just below the bump at the back of the head; the Atlas Axis Point, at the angle shown in the diagram.

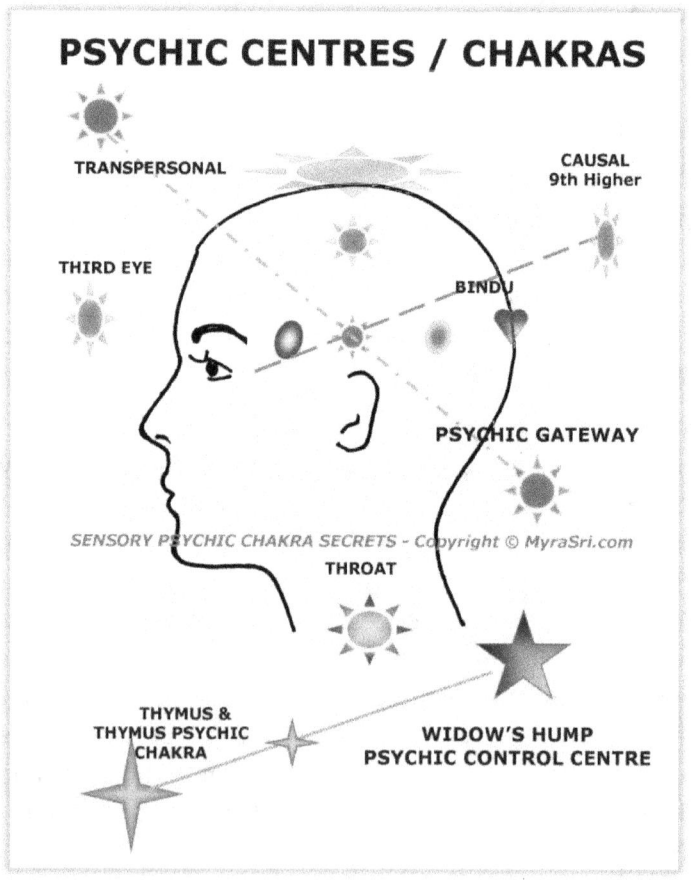

PSYCHIC CONTROL CENTRE

Back of the Neck Connection Point

There is a point on the spine at the base of the neck that sits parallel to the shoulder line and is often referred to as the "Widow's Hump". Sometimes labelled the 4 ½ Chakra or Zeal Point, as it is so close to the back of the Throat and Thymus I am not surprised that there has been some confusion as to its proper function. It sits at the junction of Cervical 7 and Thoracic 1 (C7-T1). Imagine someone getting hold of one by the "scruff of the neck" and you have the spot.

This is a Psychic Gateway point and is a major Psychic Control Point.

Others can affect this point if they have a desire to control – consider when someone comes up from behind and pats one on this area in a way that appears friendly but can actually transfer codes or negative dumpings that contain energy contrary to that which they may be attempting to portray – I have been caught out with this until I discovered the results and learned to be aware not to let someone I didn't trust touch this point – *and* how to clear myself.

Someone wanting to hang onto one, to their energy or their abilities can be registered energetically here. If one comes up and places their hand here, they may leave some form of energy cord or connection. This is a commonplace for a person wishing to hold another in compliance. One time I found someone had a claw hanging into this centre, placed there energetically by someone wanting to restrain and control them, and (wanting) to take their energy and belongings.

It can also be utilised by one as an "escape route" when one's Soul is under huge stress or in shock such as when in an accident or in great pain.

Access / Contact Point

Contact can be directly on the skin. The **best** and cleanest contact position to test I have found to be 8-15cms away from the back of the neck. Pay attention to clear any imprints, energy or codings etc that are here.

The Highly Sensitives Guide to Sensory Psychic Chakras

PSYCHIC CHAKRAS; THE BODY

Whichever way we approach the Sensory Psychic Chakras, it remains that all components of the human energy system are somehow and in many ways interrelated to each other, and these parts or aspects communicate with each other. However, the Out-of Body connections that have been observed are usually at Junction or *Connection Points* (Chakras with energy fields etc) which give rise to their own individual energy centres (at these positions). Here is how the Psychic Body anatomy below the head looked in 2009. These were all that I could track at that time and they appeared to be linked or superimposed in the same locations as existing in-body (internal) Chakras – you may recognise some of them:

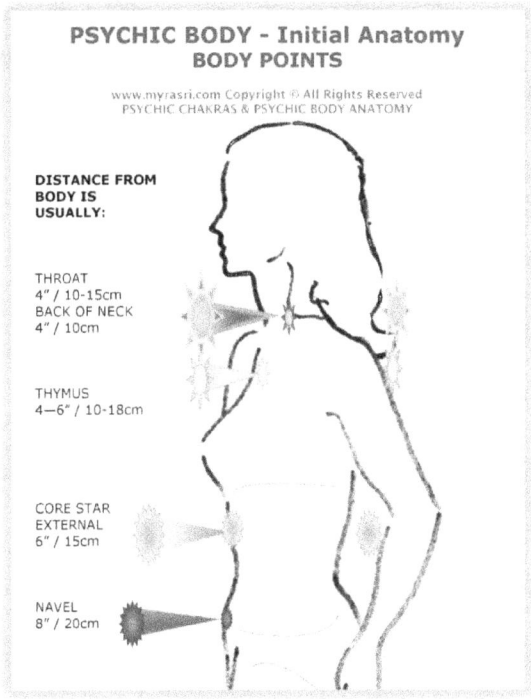

There may well be invisible lines of connections and some intereaction to the Main In-Body or other existing Chakras from these external Access / Contact Points, but the point of Power or Balance would actually be in the external Points that have been identified here.

Don't forget that these Connection Points help outline the Psychic Body itself, though as mentioned previously, it is not necessarily a neat egg shape all over.

When these Chakras emerge from the body in this manner, they are easily and best accessed via their external position – one does not need to touch the actual body that aligns along its pathway – the Contact Point will contact and connect with the whole of the particular Chakra, including its bio-locational origin and its full projection position. Though some of the Psychic Chakras may appear to occupy positions similar to the Main Chakras, or even part of the Hara system - do not assume that they are indeed the same Chakra. They just happen to occupy similar space positions but usually and often on different levels, different energetic dimensions and in different energy bodies.

However, some Chakras are Key Chakras (or Master Chakras) and act as important links or connecting points to several systems.

To Summarise; Chakras from other energy systems *can* co-exist, but they have their own particular purposes and functions; the Psychic Body Chakras, Hara system, the Main Chakras and the Signal Chakras all have separate tasks.

As we have already looked at the head and brain Chakras, let us consider the Chakras that make up the Psychic Chakra body on or around the body which include:

- The Throat Connection Point
- Back of the Neck Connection Point
- Core Star Connection Point, front and rear
- The Navel Connection Point

The Throat Connection Point

The Throat Chakra is related to the ability to communicate, and in the psychic sense, this is related to the ability to give language to one's sensory perceptions and understandings. It provides a link of energetic to verbal interpretation to what is perceived symbolically. Psychic control from another can inhibit this area.

The Connection Point can also indicate whether there is balanced communication with other areas of the Psychic Body.

Thymus Chakra

The Thymus Chakra sits below the throat and just below the sterna notch on the upper chest. It is connected to a variety of functions in its activity as a Chakra. Not considered as part of the Main Chakras, nevertheless, as a Gland Chakra it is related to supporting the Immune System; this also echoes on a Sensory Psychic level to our ability to protect ourselves on an energetic level.

The Thymus level also connects with the etheric veiling of the Psychic Body around 10-16cms from the body. This is where the best energetic connection can be accessed.

CORE STAR CONNECTION POINT,

The Core Star Chakra (front & rear) is part of the Soul Body and links to interact with the Sensory Psychic Body and other energy bodies. It acts as an integration point for psychic information, data, experiences and conflict. Rebalancing this so that one may better access one's own Core energy and resources without overlays or impact from others (and their psychic intent) helps to maintain its integrity. Old, buried or unresolved issues may impact or progress through to the back of the Core Star Chakra, affecting the middle or small of the back.

Keywords are: *Soul Expression, Integration, Integrity*

Access / Contact Point

The **best** and cleanest contact position to test would be 12-18cms away from the centre torso point.

The Navel Connection Point

The Navel is a Major Connection Point with other Energetic systems. Past psychic experiences or connections may be accessed here, and new psychic connections may be created here. Identity and dependency issues may be located here, which can compromise our ability to correctly discern and disseminate incoming data and information.

Unresolved or buried issues may affect the lower spine and one's sense of foundations, as this point is also a connection point for the Soul Body. Family and genetic issues may also be indicated. Its keywords are: *Knowing, Nurturing*

Access / Contact Point

Contact position to test would be 15-23cms out from the navel.

MASTER GATEWAY CHAKRAS

The new Gateway Chakras were the latest Psychic Chakras to be discovered. These are vital Chakras in the Sensory Chakra Anatomy and are all externalised Contact Point Chakras – they may or may not be connected to another internal Chakra but as with the others, they exist in their own right and have their own unique function.

- Psychic Gateway ; C7-T1
- Shoulder Transducer Chakras
- Spatial Chakras
- Mid-Shins Chakra

We have classified them as such because they are major energetic gateways to other energy fields and a variety of energies, vibrations, memories, records, data, realms and dimensions. There are other Advanced Master Gateway Chakras not yet ready to share generally publicly but available to those ready for them.

On a more day-to-day level, these Gateways act as the governing Out-of-Body Centres that interface with the energetic environment and are actually vital to sensory, psychic and physical function.

The first new Gateways to be discovered were the **Shoulder Chakras**. The second set are called the **Spatial** Chakras. These are **Gateway Chakras**, along with the Psychic Point (Back of the Neck) and the Master or Psychic Centres in the Brain. Later came the **Shin Chakras**.

CARE With Energy Input!!

A Cautionary Note here:

Channelling of psychic energy is usually via the Gateway centres, though not necessarily absolutely always.

There are many forms of channelling, and this book does not cover mediumship except in the case of one channelling their Higher Self or Higher Soul, which is enhanced through addressing the Chakras in this book.

A variety of energies and a variety of dimensions, planes of existence, astral levels and paranormal dens and denizens exist. Identifying or recognition before accessing or surrendering to certain energies is important to keep one's energy systems safe; and to preserve the integrity of the Soul and the Spiritual Agenda held therein. The Dark has had plenty of experience in portraying itself as a form of Light... So test and challenge the fruits of any professed "Light Worker", Light-Bearer or incoming Entity as the Astral Planes are crowded with pseudo "Masters", Arch-Angels, "Red Eagles" or whatevers... Working on this level will only give you a certain understanding and will in actual fact prevent you in going through to your own Soul Source. Always be mindful when considering an Energy Source or Entity...

Even energy workers can be caught out by an incompatible energetic system that proclaims great results but is fraught with "follow-me" hooks and low-grade information dressed as fancy glam words and advertising. Hook it up with energy manipulation, and it's hard to see clearly that temporary results are not true healing that has registered on a Soul Level – the true grounding and anchoring place for long-term healing. We have seen others, even the well-advertised, delivering limiting information disguised as the latest mastery techniques. Self proclamation and belief and the semi-hypnotised "recommendations" of devotees does not change the nature of the energy (and personal agenda) that they channel.

But to each their own. And different stories can be played out in the background of our learnings; karmic lessons to be re-taken if not learned the first time around, opportunities for clearing past life debts; a final releasing of those who intend to change but cannot, and other such stories.

Buyer Beware

Integrity is a much bandied about word. Most of us understand that this usually means that one is living in accord with moral and ethical principles, that there is a soundness of moral character. However, there *are* other meanings to the same word.

Another meaning, one which is often overlooked by others yet is spot on; is the state of being whole, of being integrated, inter-grated, of being entire, undivided, all parts agreeing. This means that what is within the being, person or thing, then this state is congruent with what they do externally. When a person I knew kept using this word "Integrity" regarding himself and all of his personal and business relationships, and he later proved to be a con-artist, liar, cheat and narcissist, I had to challenge this self-description (naturally). Talking about this with one smart person, I did a rethink when they said that he actually *was* in integrity... he had the integrity of a snake... Examining this further I realised that he was a snake; he had acted like one, sneaked in like one, attacked like one, poisoned everything like one and had slithered away like one.

So challenging who and what and learning toward learning discernment is important when it comes to personal matters, trust and the allowing of inclusion.

Incompatible Energies

Importance must be placed on working only with the correct compatible vibrational initiations or activations, as some that have come up against ones dis-resonant to who they are on a Soul Level have been known to experience; Psychic Aberrations, Psychic Shock, Psychotic Episodes or Psychosis and even Psychic Madness - when a vibration or frequency that is too strong, too alien, has a string of darkness attached, holds hidden agendas or is driven by force or ego impacts them.

One client who had experienced a *Shakti-Pat* – an energetic initiation, Kundalini activation and energy transference by a "Master" – took *years* to recover from the ensuing damage; their kundalini energy shot through to the Crown Chakra creating short-circuiting along the way as the process was "forced" rather than a gradual owning and understanding through each Chakra. They were energetically burnt-out before they had started, though the initial euphoria fooled them into thinking the process had been other than safe. In another instance a Reiki client collapsed after her Master trainings and process – this energy Initiation totally drained and unbalanced her and she was unable to do any more energy work for many years; when we checked we found that the Reiki energies were totally incompatible with her. The Reiki Symbols used also limited and restricted the flow of chi at each sealed point, and her "Master" had set it up that a portion of her energy was continually syphoned off to him. Hmmmm...!

Not everyone who claims to be "good" actually is just that...

A past life historic experience of Psychic Madness, magikal manipulation or dark magic can also leave an imprint in one's psychic centres, whether one was the initiator or the impacted, and it is important to heal this and remove all related past resonances for a healthier current life function in order to navigate one's everyday occurrences as well as the increasing extra-ordinary vibrations that we currently find ourselves living in.

Shoulder Transducers Chakras

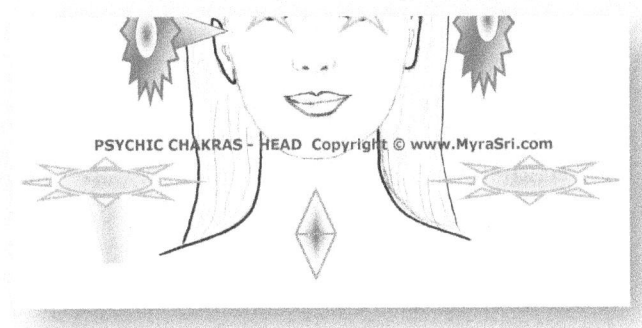

Hovering approximately 2' – 5' (5-10cm) above each shoulder, these Connection Chakra Points are **major** factors in balancing the Psychic Body.

These act as Outer-Filters and **Transducers** of energy and information; that is that they *convert* energy into a usable form. They are also important Portals as they link to the Psychic Chakra System, the Higher Chakras and the Auric Bodies. They are the first to receive galactic and cosmological information, codings, frequencies or other vibrational broadcasts.

Their key words are: *Transducing, Channelling, Receiving*

Once cleared, centred again and balanced, they seem to assist in clearing many of the other psychic channels to provide a clearer and easier flow of energy input and information. It is often one of the first general points that I check in a balance; I recommend that one always check these important positions when looking at balancing the Psychic Anatomy.

The spin on these Chakras was not initially easy to track. However, they are found to generally be like spinning orbs on a horizontal axis; similar to seeing miniature Saturns with her rings sitting horizontally above each shoulder. The energy is connected via a sort of channel that emerges from each of the shoulders themselves.

Balancing Possibilities

To balance them these are the methods I have found effective:

- Use of an indicated Essential Oil (via kinesiology, intuition, reference or pendulum) in a sweeping, wiping or clearing motion. If working with a particular issue, for further understanding of the choice of Essential Oil, refer to "*Secrets Beyond Aromatherapy*".

- Emission of Essential Oil Etherics by a static hand held in the Chakra space

- Holding of energy together with another Psychic Body Chakra (often the stomach / Navel or a another Psychic Chakra)

- Performing Figure 8 movements in different directions are effective when overwhelm or stagnation is present; most effective are horizontal movements

- Use of sound (tuning forks, cymbals etc) to break up congestion in and around the Chakras, also finger clicking if none of these are available

- Check the ears and their filters after clearing the shoulder Chakras

Access / Contact Point

Positioned horizontally approximately 2"- 5" (5-10cm) above each shoulder.

Spatial Chakras

Keyword: *"In/Out"*

Position: At approximately breast or chest nipple height and at an angle of approximately 20° away from the midline, and about 30-50 cm distance and in line with the nipples (in both men and women) there are two Chakras concerned with a variety of functions.

These have been one of the most recent Chakras to find and identify on the Psychic Body. Their concern is to work in concert with the Aura. They have a variety of tasks, and they not only take in information, energy and stimulus into the energy fields, Psychic Body and physical body, they also release over-produced Psychic energy from within and further assist in assigning and directing Psychic energy correctly within the Psychic body and its components, and ultimately help maintain balance in the human physical vehicle.

These are also **Regulator** Chakras and a major function is growth and development. It is a major Psychic Gateway. It also links and connects with the back of the neck Psychic Point.

The Spatial Chakras can also connect to Past Life Karma and issues as it feeds into the Soul Body and Causal Body and back again as part of its duties with communication and interpretation.

These Master Chakras also link to the Emotional and Etheric Bodies.

Access / Contact Point

About 30-50 cm away from the breasts or nipples, angled at 20° from centre.

Mid-Shins Chakras

Keyword: *Stability, Direction*

This is the Psychic Chakra for **Stability**, and I often call is as such as it regulates stability. It helps to hold the Psychic Body steady and unwavering when an influx of energies may unbalance it. You might view it as a kind of anchor point, and it aids to connect the Psychic Body to the Soul Body and Astral Body. Its Keyword is Direction and it is also concerned with Stability issues. This Chakra is multi-directional.

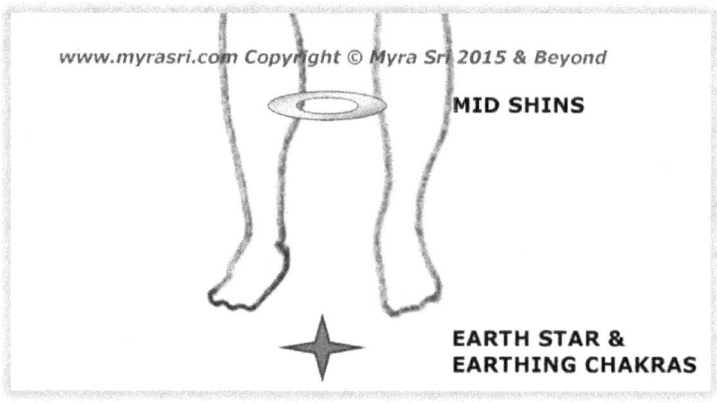

Access / Contact Point

Its position is located between and just slightly to the front of the middle of the Shins.

Psychic Body Chakra Links – Connection Points

It is clear that sensory psychic anatomy has changed since first documenting the various points and Chakras. The current picture incorporates these newer access areas.

Our Sensory Psychic Anatomy is an energetic body, with various unique and specific Connection Points located at various positions related to the areas and functions that they are connected with. We discovered various sensitive points along the surface of the Psychic Body and when these are indicated as requiring attention, they can often also signal a related dis-function to the area involved.

The illustration following this section shows various Light Body Connection Points with both Centre-line Chakras and outside limb minor Psychic Chakras.

These are all responsible for signalling and transmitting information (to a lesser degree than the Master Psychic Chakras) for sensory and date interpretation.

These energy centres can be affected, un-balanced, impacted or misplaced through trauma, negative energies or accident, and this can have an effect on the overall functioning, though to a lesser degree than the other more major Chakras. However, they are important in that they help to keep the body aligned and in the right space location, and to prevent forms of disorientation which tend to distort perceptions and may result in faulty readouts of incoming information (which can affect balance and movement).

They may be seen as light points and when they are imbalanced, they affect function, twist the energy centres or allow interference that can taint or confuse.

If all else shows clear during an energy healing, but there is an issue in the Psychic Body, then it is worth checking these points out. Sometimes it's as simple as a message about a person or place that is inharmonious in frequency. Other times, it may simply be an elemental energy that has become caught up in the psychic anatomy in some way.

You will see by the Psychic Body Chakra List that there are issues that can cause imbalance in the system that are not necessarily from an obvious or dramatic cause.

Access / Contact Points

These points vary depending on their position and on their current state though a general rule is that they are contactable on the body to a distance of about 4" or 10cm. Some points are safe to access by touch directly on the body (usually over clothing if present) such as the hands and feet, which can be accessed by touching the soles and palms. The side points – knees, ankles, elbows etc – can range from body surface to as far as 10cms or more away from the body.

The Contact Points for the Throat, Thymus, Back of the Neck Point, Core Star, and Navel may radiate from between 10-20 cms out from the body or as previously listed.

The keywords and functions for these are included in the Psychic Chakra List that follows in the next chapter.

The Highly Sensitives Guide to Sensory Psychic Chakras

WORKING WITH THE NEW CHAKRAS

INCLUDES:

LIST OF CHAKRAS SUMMARY

PREPARING TO WORK ENERGETICALLY
CLEAR AND ENERGISED

PSYCHIC CORE ENERGISE EXERCISE

LIGHT CHANNEL CLEARANCE

FILTERS & BLOCKAGES

TOOLS FOR BALANCING

AFFIRMATIONS, CHALLENGES

SOUL REGISTRATION

CASE HISTORIES

PRIMARY POINTS

SUMMARY - Psychic Body Chakra List

Here is a listing of the Psychic Body Chakras and Connections for ease of reference:

Psychic Centres In Brain

- Guru
- Ajna
- Soma
- Manas
- Bindu

Centre / Mid Line; Front

- Crown (Pituitary/Hypothalamus/Pineal)
    - *Channelling*
- Transpersonal (Pineal)
    - *Communicating, Interpreting*
- Third Eye-s (Inner and Outer) (Pineal/Pituitary, Kidneys, Spleen)
    - *Visioning*
- Mouth (Link To Throat, Nervous System, Amygdala)
    - *Prophesying, Affirming*
- Nose (Olfactory and Psychic Centres)
    - *Sniffing-Out, Knowing*
- Throat (Nervous System, Throat);
    - *Prophesying, Language*
- Thymus
    - *Healing, Safety, Self Love,*
- High Heart, Solar Plexus
    - *Channelling, Love*

- Core Star – Soul Body
  - *Soul Expression, Integration*
- Navel (Major Connection Point for several Energetic systems)
  - *Knowing, Nurturing*
- Mid-Shins (Gateway)
  - *Direction, Stability*
- Earth Star, Earthing Chakras
  - *Grounding, Anchoring, Reality*

Centre Line; Back

- Causal Chakra – 9th Upper Chakra
  - *Connection Point to Soul and Mind*
- Psychic Gateway Point / Back Atlas-Neck
  - *Access and Escape Point, Healing, Autonomy*
- Psychic Control Point
  - *Back Access Control Centre*
- Heart
  - *Access Point, Back Entry*

Side

- Horns Left and Right (Link To Throat, Heart, Stomach)
  - *Accessing*
- Eyes (Link To Heart and Throat - and Lungs)
  - *Visioning*
- Ears and Inner Ear Filters (Link To Heart, Throat and Solar Plexus)
  - *Input*
- **Shoulder** Outer Filters **Transducer** / Portals (Gateway) : Links To Chakra System, Higher Chakras and Auric Bodies)- First To Receive Galactic Or Other Broadcasts
  - *Transducing, Channelling, Receiving*

Out-of-Body Chakras; Pairs

Generally related to Boundaries, our personal Space, our ability to relate to others and to life.

- Top of Arm / Side Shoulder – *Teamwork, Shared Goals or Values*
- Outer Elbow – *Boundaries, Safety, Guarding*
- Hands – *Major sensors and interpreters in touch and energy*
- Outer Knees – *Strength and humility in direction and movement*
- Outer Ankles – *Flexibility in direction and movement*
- Soles of Feet – *Standing our ground, Walking our path, Earth empathy*
- SPATIAL Chakras (Gateway) – *Breast Level – In/Out, Governing, Feedback, Release*

Skin and Hair:

- *Receptors - Warning or Confirmation*

Multi-Function Chakras

Both of the Eyes and Ear Chakras as well as the Mouth Chakra exist in other Chakra or Energetic Systems.

To ensure you are working with a Sensory Chakra (the Psychic anatomy), when performing a scan or identification / diagnosis in a normal healing session, just check to see which system you are actually working with – physical, energetic body, meridian etc – to further support your understanding of the issues involved and to enhance the efficacy.

If the point includes another system as well, include that in your balance. You may well find correlations.

WORKING WITH THE NEW CHAKRAS

Some preparation is required to work with your New Chakras. Getting as balanced and ready as much as possible is important for clearer work and the best results. Particularly if you are working on a client.

Some of these techniques can also assist you in self-alignment at any time and for other situations.

1. Preparation; Neutrality, Psychic Core prepared, Light Channels cleared
2. Assess or Note current state *before* performing clearings
3. Clear the Psychic Chakras using the recommended Tools; Initial Clearing should include all Chakras and Connection Points, usually working from the head down. There is a Balance / Correction Sheet included in the *Balancing the Chakras* Section.
4. Always attend to *Soul Registration* of the changes at the end of each session or major segment – see *Soul Registration* Section and definitely at the end of the session work
5. Reassess or re-note the state or condition *after* clearing for comparison and completion
6. If there is a particular theme during the experience, decide what further ongoing action is necessary, or design an affirmation or mind-state to focus on to support the new direction
7. Subsequent clearings can utilise a check of specific Primary Points. This may avoid the need for a full check through of all Psychic Chakras again, as some will still be managing okay (depending on other factors)

Preparing to work with the New Chakras

Steps of Preparation:
1. Assess your current – *before* - condition
2. Prepare the Psychic CORE
3. Check your Light Channels and clear any Blockages
4. Check Light Channel Filters
5. Assess your *after* condition or state
6. You are ready to work – remember to check and clear any other Filters you come across along the way

Assessment
If you can find a way to assess your state, your feelings or sense of things *before* you do any of the steps and especially after completing different portions of the Psychic anatomy, and you repeat this assessment or note-taking again *after* then you will have a measure, a standard to recheck against at the end of the session. This gives you and your energy systems positive feedback, and this helps to remind them of what is possible again. You can use any barometer; a rating of 10 out of 10, say, with 10 being the worst you have ever felt or experienced on that issue. Or if you have kinesiology or dowsing skills you can use a percentage check.

Prepare the CORE
We recommend the Psychic CORE Toner exercise to ensure that your Core is clear, or at least that there are no blockages for the free flow of energy. You may wish to use a Hara Line exercise if you know one, instead, but there is a difference. The instructions for the Psychic CORE Toner exercise are listed in the "Tools" Section.

Clear the Light Channels

To access better access to one's own Light Source, and to assist in clearing energy channels in the head and the Crown Chakra, this exercise is strongly recommended. Instructions to clear are provided in the *Tools* Section.

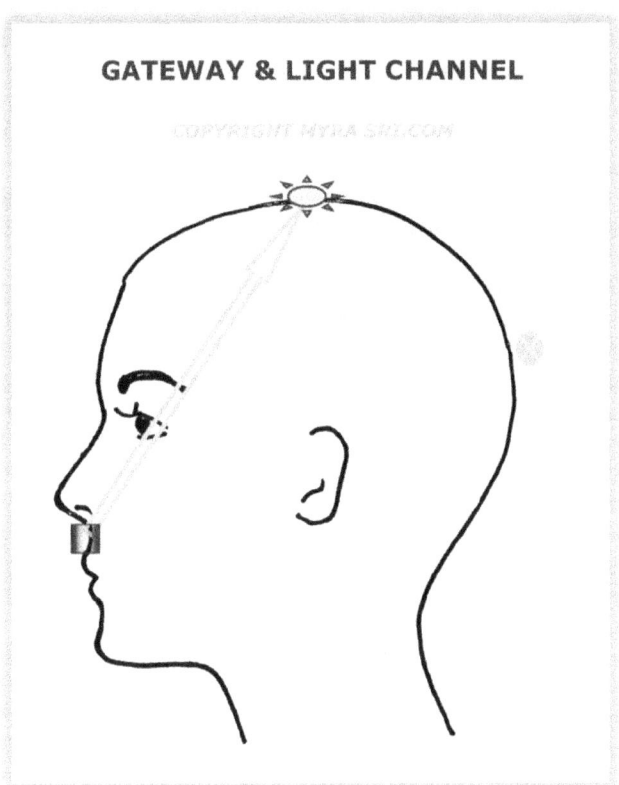

Above is an illustration of one form of Light Channel; a channel of Light.

The exercises and instructions to clear Light Channels in the head are given in the *"Tools"* Section.

Psychic Body CORE Foundation

Middle Pillar-Core

First things first. As mentioned earlier, let's look at getting the foundations right. In my workshops on these Chakras, I guide my students through a process to ensure that their Central Core Chanel is clear and activated before proceeding to diagnose and balance these Chakras or its system. This exercise is important and wise for both clients or practitioners or simply for self balance. It will ensure correct connection to one's true Spiritual Source which aids to reduce error, ensure neutrality, and allow the highest results.

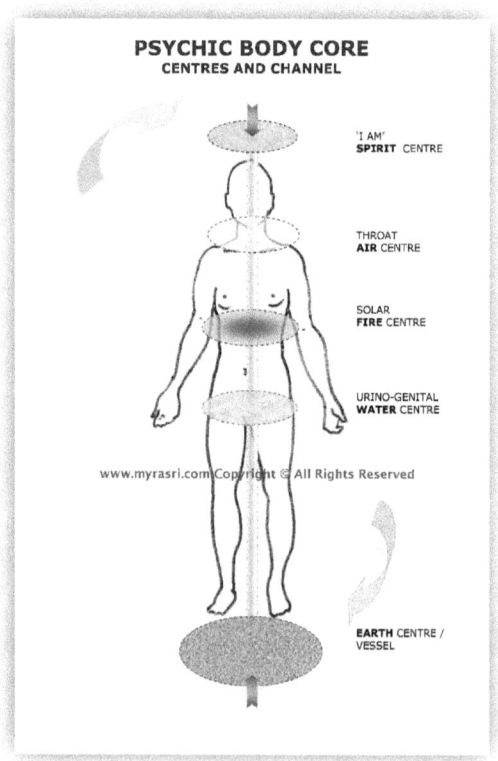

*The exercise that I use to clear and strengthen the Central Channel is the **Psychic Toner Exercise**. This exercise is included in my book "Secrets Behind Energy Fields" and is part of the **New Evolved Chakras Workbook series**. It is also available as a Guided Meditation; **Psychic CORE Toner**.*

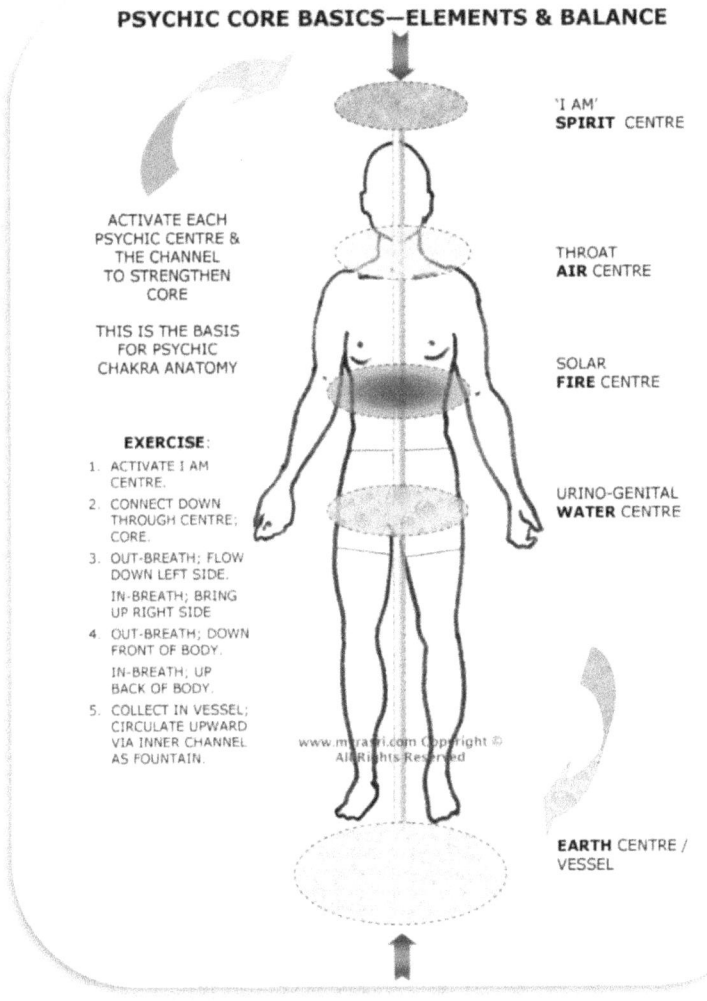

This exercise clears the main energy channel through the body with cleansing energy using the breath.

The full instructions are included in the *Tools* Section.

It also sets the main elemental energy centres in the body, and these are fired up to support the light bodies and aura. This is then best followed by clearing the Light channels in the head. The instructions for this is in the Section; **"Preparing to Work with the Chakras"**.

Balance & Calibrate the Psychic Body

There are a variety of methods that can be used to clear, balance and align these Chakras.

For some people Activation may begin as soon as they see a picture of them... Those that are somewhat more advanced or energetically evolved may find that looking at one of the pictures can trigger an action (or reaction) in a Chakra; and this may be because the Chakra required this visual symbolic input of information.

A part of us is always wanting to heal itself, and a visual message can be sufficient to begin the process, particularly for the Sensory body which has direct input into the visual and sensory mechanisms, for it acknowledges in a more observable concrete or viewable form that which it recognises *should* be, and the energy systems then set about sorting this out through its desire to be whole again.

To work with the Psychic anatomy, and as stated elsewhere, always first start off with familiarising oneself with one's Core – the Psychic Toner Core Exercise assists in this.

Check the Preparation list in "Preparing to Work with the New Chakras". Then either scan the energy bodies as illustrated, or for the first time, follow the Psychic Body Chakra List.

Clean and balance the Chakra Connection Points using any of the methods in *Balancing Techniques and Tools*. We have found that the most effective healing tool is to track back in time.

The Most Effective Methods:
Track back to the original time and source of the problem that caused the imbalance; find and clear the cause energetically.

Settle, clear and clean up the Connection Point or Chakra; use energy work, the breath, essential oils, affirmations and support.

Feel for a smooth flow in the energies, clearing, aligning and recalibrating as you go.

Reconnect to the appropriate links as suggested. Once the Psychic Body Chakras have been balanced and aligned totally, and the Shoulder Transducers and Master Chakras set or reset, it is a much easier matter for the next balancing session. For having aligned all of the Psychic anatomy, the next occasion that there appears to be a possible problem or issue, one can go straight to the Master or Gateway Chakras to check for an indication that the issue lies in the Psychic body.

Recalibration simply means aligning the range of frequencies to be compatible with the Soul of the person, and that the total energetic and frequency alignment of their Sensory Psychic anatomy now agrees with current energy frequencies and that they line up or interface in a harmonious and supportive way.

Recalibration Challenge Statement;
"This ... Chakra is now cleared and calibrated to the correct and appropriate frequency to enable optimal function and efficiency, safely, completely and easily."

Soul Registration

A primary consideration is that at the end of all healings, or major junctures in healing, one ensures that:

For a healing or balance to be lasting and effective, all healings and changes are to be locked-in or registered at the Soul level...

The Soul Body is now involved with the healing process; this is to ensure that the essence of the client's *totality* of being has *acknowledged* the positive changes and *registers* them in order to *integrate* the healing; and to further align and support the Soul's ongoing journey.

This is usually done via the Soul Star Chakra, which is the Soul's Individuation point.

Though the Soul Core Star may also be included where required. This locking-in and acknowledgement also allows any aspects of the original issue that impinged upon the Soul prior to the balance or healing to now flow through to a completion or release; the resulting resolution can now assist in a healing for the Soul. As the Soul is that part of the Being which registers and continues the journey and travels of all of its incarnations, it is fitting that the Soul is considered and assured with each healing.

Soul Records can then be re-ordered and what has been dealt with can be "taken off the table". Other priorities can be re-considered if or where necessary and other choices or options be presented.

If there is difficulty in completing this registration, then it may indicate that there are other issues involved that require attention or clearing so that the Soul can fully register the change.

"My Soul, body and being now 100% accepts this balance and healing, easily and safely"

"I now 100% integrate and retain ALL of the benefits of this balance for my Highest Good and in alignment with my own True Soul Purpose and Destiny"

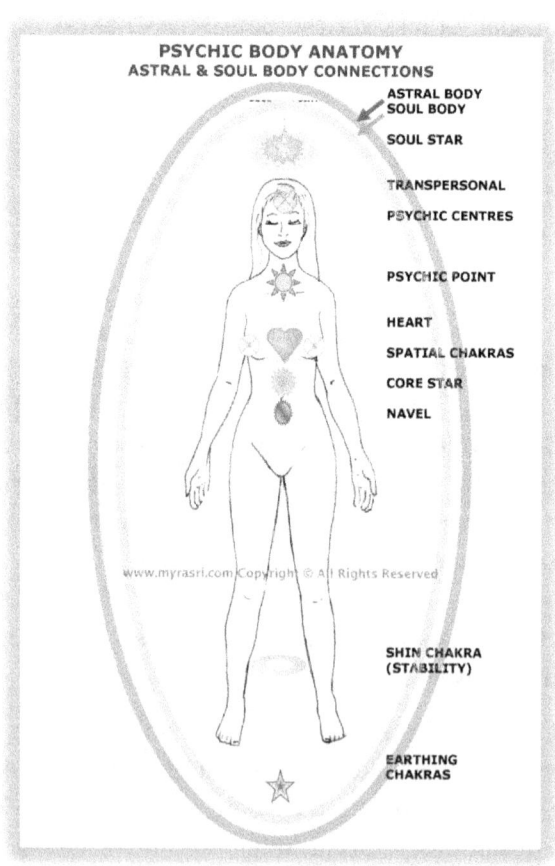

TOOLS for Working with the New Chakras

Some ideas for balancing have been provided with the descriptions of a particular Chakra.

There are also **Affirmations** that can be used as "Challenge Statements" – this means that saying them our loud can reveal if there is anything other than a complete agreement with the statement can become revealed. Kinesiology barometer ratings such as the ascertaining of what percentage still remains to be cleared before the statement or Challenge rings totally true energetically are revealing. (The easy and simple technique to teach yourself how to self-test is shared in my *"Secrets Behind Energy Fields"* book.) Dowsing or internal intuiting – if you know how to do such things – can also reveal an untrue statement.

For those of you who are not familiar with such Tools, then using your own inner sensing (which strengthens with practise, I assure you) can reveal much to you. If there is an even flow with a statement, no sense of inhibition, discomfort. pain, inkling or hesitation, but simply strong assurance felt within, then that is the perfect self tool to guide you on your way.

Tracking Back: To really balance a Chakra, or indeed, any part of a being, their body or their subtle body anatomy, it is always important to trace back to the cause of the problem. If there is a reason why a Chakra is not functioning, even though it is present in the new subtle body anatomy, one can track back to the time when it was disabled or interfered with, or when the problem first started. This may also point to the circumstances or to a particular event or person implicit in the issue. Or it can point to time of challenge or stress for the client that impacted on the development of the particular Chakra. This is vital information. It is also freeing information. The truth can set you free. For now one can decide what to do with the information, and with the impact of the original cause.

Clearing the Light Channels in the head is essential for clear self connection. From time to time check on any **Filters** you may have encountered.

Energising the **Psychic CORE** is important to establish a clearing and a strengthening before attending to each or any of the Psychic Chakras – initially… and it is also good practise to regularly clear and energise your sensory apparatus in a general way.

Vibrational solutions and suggestions are also included here.

Importance of **Soul Registration** and how to do that are listed.

Recalibration instructions for a Chakra are provided.

Some suggestions for follow-up Sensory balances are listed in the **Primary Points** Section.

For quick location of a problem in the Sensory body, you can do a **Body Scan**. This is simply the use of imagination or visualisation to pinpoint any discrepancies in the anatomy. Close your eyes and imagine yourself standing in front of you, or see a picture of yourself up on a screen. Now working slowly downwards, look to check any areas that seem cloudy, dark, twisted or not quite right in any other way. When you are focussing on the position where a Chakra could possibly be located (and waiting for alignment or activation etc) you can use the same technique. Another way to do this is to be aware of the tone or feel in the palm of your hand, and then slowly and gently pass the palm around the head and over the body, feeling with the palm (and your own inner sense of ok-ness) for any extra heat, cold, agitation, or sense of discrepancy.

A basic **Balance or Correction Sheet** has been included for those who wish to track their efforts and improvements. You are welcome to adapt this to suit your needs.

Psychic CORE Toner Exercise

This is also available as an mp3 Guided Meditation on The Instructions for the Psychic CORE Toner Exercise are provided here.

Each of us has our own Auric & Psychic shield. Each person's energy field is of a different strength, vibration & density. Depending on our life experiences, our beliefs, our experiences & our life purposes, we will each have a different expression of innate self-protection in our subtle body fields & shields. Please understand & honour those different needs & focus on what is best for you.

1. Centre & ground yourself sitting or standing
2. Imagine a sphere of brilliant white light above the crown of your head. This sphere should be viewed as being active & abundantly alive with energy; it is your **Spirit** Centre and the key to your true self. Vibrate the words "I Am" like a mantra while maintaining this visualisation
3. After allowing your mind to rest here for five minutes, imagine your Spirit Centre sends out a shaft of white light down through your skull & brain, continuing until it stops at your Throat and expands to form another sphere of brilliant white light. This is your **Air** centre, related to Saturn. Focus on this vital sphere
4. After allowing your mind to rest here for five minutes, imagine your Air Centre sends out a shaft of white light down through your body until it reaches your Solar Plexus and expands to form another sphere of brilliant white light. This is your **Fire** centre, related to the Sun. Focus on this energy in this active sphere

5. After allowing your mind to rest here for five minutes, imagine your Fire Centre sends out a shaft of white light down through until it arrives at your Genital region, and expands to form another sphere of brilliant white light. This is your **Water** centre, related to the Moon. Focus on this sphere
6. After allowing your mind to rest here for five minutes, imagine your Water Centre sends out a shaft of white light down through your body until it reaches your Feet where it expands to form a final sphere of brilliant white light. This is your **Earth** centre, related to powers associated with the Earth, such as food, clothing & shelter. Focus on this sphere of solidity for five minutes
7. Focus your attention on your Spirit Centre and imagine it vigorously absorbing spiritual energy from the atmosphere around you. Exhale & visualise this energy flowing down the left side of your body. Inhale and visualise this same energy flowing under your feet and up the right side of your body to return to your Spirit Centre. Notice that this energy is inside all of your bodies, both visible and invisible. Keep this visualisation going until the energy has completed at least six full circuits
8. Imagine that this energy flows from your Spirit Centre down the front of your body to your feet as you exhale, and then flows under your feet and up the back of your body to return to your Spirit Centre as you inhale. Continue this visualisation until at least six full circuits have been completed
9. Send your attention down to your Earth Centre. This must be viewed as a vessel containing all power. Imagine that your Spirit Centre is drawing this power up to it as you inhale in such a way that it fountains up out of your Spirit Centre, and then,

as you exhale, it falls down all around your body until it collects again in the vessel that your Earth Centre has become. Visualise at least six of these fountain-ing circulations of power.

This Exercise sets your Psychic energy and assists with creating a strong Psychic shield.

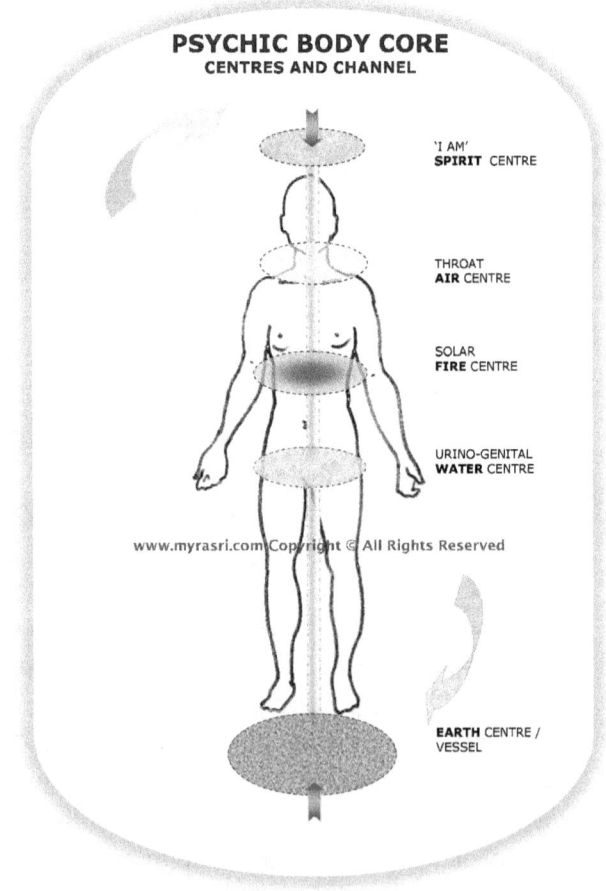

LIGHT CHANNELs

Connection to Your True Source

After we have ensured that the Psychic CORE Channel is energised, we establish the link to the Crown Chakra – a connection that is separate from the linking through the Main Chakra system. This pathway helps establish a Spiritual linkage and can further support the conduit and flow into the Main Chakra, sometimes taking their resonance to a higher level - though not always, as this is dependent on the person and the work that they have undertaken on themselves and on their energy bodies.

There are **two possible pathways** to this point, as not every Soul has the same connection depending on their purpose and history. Whichever one you find as you work in this area, we affirm that this clearing and establishing is helpful to support the Pathway for Light and further enables correct Access to Divine Source.

Indentify which pathway fits your anatomy and clear these conduits by following the Channels of Light and further infuse with Light via the focused breath.

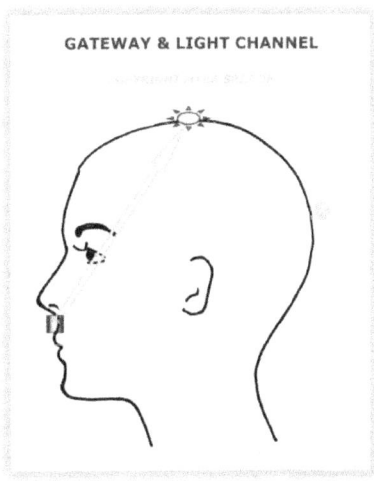

GATEWAY & LIGHT CHANNEL

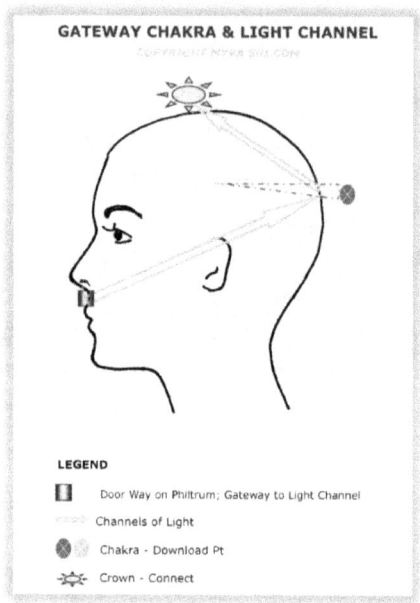

Both pathways lead to the Crown Chakra, and help establish correct tone within the head space. Both are valid and just denote differing Soul Experience and history.

As you clear you may encounter some blockages which

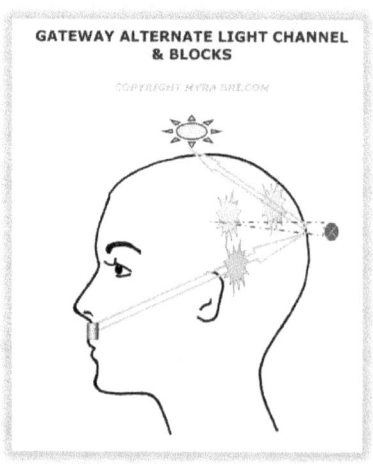

you can clear and filters which you can clean.

Filters & Blockages

Locate any filters and ensure that they are cleaned and cleared. Blockages need to be cleared out too.

Filters can become gummed up through toxic or psychic gunk or be overwhelmed with others energies.

A quick guided meditation on this should be available

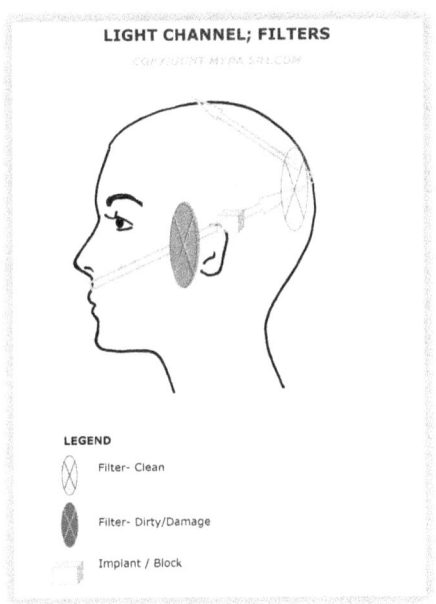

midyear 2017 on

To clear any filters, one has to gently slowly remove and cleanse these in Light before replacing. The original position of the filter must also be cleansed before returning.

Recommended Essential Oils

Essential Oils have their own unique colour codes which governs the actions of the specific oil. Their role in the current New Era Energies includes the New Chakras.

Because they possess a vibrational frequency that can interact with the nervous system, the brain and our Sensory apparatus quickly and easily, they are extremely effective for clearing and alignment support.

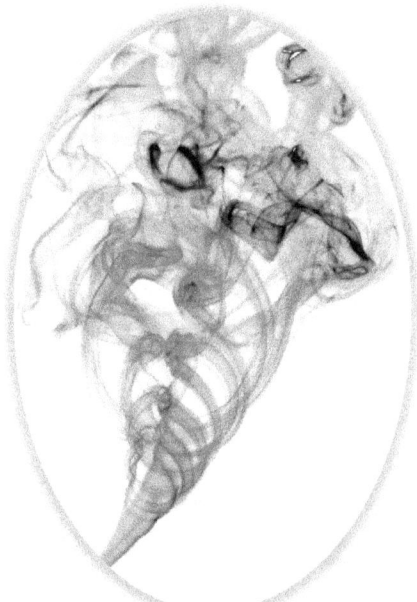

Some suggestions of **Essential Oils** include:

One can draw the Essential Oil energy into the visual areas with imagination, my breathe technique (my *Secrets Beyond Aromatherapy* book) or by intention, in order to clean and clear along the entire optical nerve system.

Dispose of any used tissues safely and hygienically as the tissue will have gathered toxic or negative etheric phlegm or psychic plasma. (References given are from *Secrets Beyond Aromatherapy.*)

Recommended for Eye Chakras, Ear Chakras, Crown Chakra, Master Gateway Chakras and any other indicated Chakra. *Do not use directly on skin, but Aurically.*

Frankincense:

"Spiritual Purpose...", "Crown, Third Eye...the Light Body", "...transitions...", "strengthening ... the Higher Chakras..."

Lavender:

"Aligning the Major Chakras...", "...allows for new intuitive information...", "help soothe the Soul and strengthen the auric and subtle bodies to further hold the rebalanced energies", "stronger sense of connection with guidance or the Angelic realm".

Lemongrass:

"Pessimism can be eased... the brain can open pathways and clearer thinking can be generated", "...to cleanse and strengthen the astral body", "...a tonic to the etheric body and aura", "...Crown Chakra", "...repairs auric holes...nervous system calmed...".

Rose:

"Rainbow energies of Light...", "...settles energetic interruptions", "allow energy of Spirit to provide protection", "higher vibration is easier to assimilate into the auric fields".

Note:

Great for clearing energy crap from **Skin** and **Hair**.

Other Vibrational Essences

Possible Indicated **Essences** that I have found suitable or effective at the time and thus can recommend include:

Shell Essences;

- Just Me
- I Am

AuraSoma Vibrational Essences;

- White Pomander
- Lord Metatron
- Deep Magenta

Flower Essences;

- Fringed Violet
- Angelsword

There are other essences that are also suitable. Check your stock and use what emerges as appropriate at the time.

AFFIRMATIONS:

Here you will find proven Affirmations for your added ease of quick reference. They can also be used as statements to "Challenge" the true state of a Chakra...

Soul Healing Registration

The Soul requires recognition and consideration in all healing processes, and it is necessary that the Soul accepts and is party to the positive changes therein. It is vital that the Soul registers the changes. This can be done as the important "LOCK-IN" procedure for the end of EVERY session or healing, to ensure full and accepted benefit by balancing the following;

"My Soul, body and being now 100% accepts this balance and healing, easily and safely"

"I now 100% integrate and retain ALL of the benefits of this balance for my Highest Good and in alignment with my own True Soul Purpose and Destiny"

Clearing Affirmations

"My body consciousness, my psychic anatomy, my total energy systems now 100% refuse to take on board or to process any and all chemicals from Chemtrails or from related toxic release or spillage, so be it"

"I reclaim my own separate anatomy from the world at large; I resist safely, easily, elegantly any attempts to subdue me, my body, my mind and my journey, so be it."

"I now 100% reclaim my own body at the cellular level to be safely and easily 100% free from all external pollutants. I no longer accept that which would inhibit me, and I throw it off."

"I am now 100% free from all allegiances, subscriptions, conscriptions, promises, vows or jurisdictions of .... (cult, belief or religious affiliation) from this point on and I commit allegiance only to my True Source and my Higher Purpose according to my Souls true intentions."

"I now 100% choose and have the right to choose my own Spiritual Journey, in alignment with my own Soul Purpose and Mission and Destiny. I 100% release safely and completely any and all judgments placed on me from any religion, "faith" or belief system that is contrary to my own. I allow my own Soul and my Higher Self to be in total charge of my journey, free from the control of others. So be it."

"I can be and am Spiritual without the need for religiosity or a man-made set of beliefs. I am now 100% ready to connect and work with my own True Divine Source according to my highest Soul journey and purpose."

"My Psychic centres and anatomy, my total body consciousness, my Immune System, my brain and my mind now 100% refuse acceptance of any frequencies,

broadcasts, Radionics or energy projections encoded with or carrying virus frequencies, virus codes or settings. I release totally any and all absorbed related frequencies and codes and I 100% reset back to who I truly am and to my full health again."

"Any and all toxic vibrations, energy waves or frequencies broadcast or emitted from any source that is not for my highest good and best health are now released and returned to its source, never to return to me again. so be it."

"I 100% refuse to accept any alien or harmful frequencies, any harmful virus or energetic vibrations calibrated to cause dys-function or dis-ability and I reclaim my right to nurture my own body safely again. My hair, my skin and my eyes are now conduits of Light again and all dark or dirty is released completely, safely, and immediately."

"I am 100% free from the projections, intents, pushy thoughts and judgements of others. I now easily recognise sales, media and marketing manipulation and I also willingly recognise faulty logic and quasi-reasoning."

"I now know what is a want and what is a need for me, and I have the right to my own opinion on these things without peer or family or partner or sales pressure."

"I am perfect and acceptable exactly as I am."

Psychic Chakra Affirmations

Insert the issue in the blank space to challenge any lingering or remaining energies for a full clearance.

"My Psychic Control Centre is now 100% free from any energetic hooking, any control imprinting, any attempts to use or manage me or to reduce my self-autonomy or abilities or Light and I reclaim my own control for myself again. So be it"

"This ... Chakra is now 100% clear"

"I am 100% clear from the influence of others"

"This ... Chakra is now 100% clear and ready for integration with my Psychic Body"

"This ... Chakra is now 100% safely aligned to the New Incoming frequencies"

"I now safely use my Psychic Chakras in integrity and without harm to others"

"My Psychic Chakras are now 100% free from the ... of others"

"My Psychic Anatomy is now clear and inter-connected"

My Sensory Psychic Anatomy is now fully harmonised and activated"

*"My Sensory Psychic Chakras register that which is important for **me** to know, and I can now control my energy to avoid getting mixed up in another's energy or affairs"*

"This ... Chakra is now cleared and calibrated to the correct and appropriate frequency to enable optimal function and efficiency, safely, completely and easily."

General Affirmation Ideas

"I am me myself and nobody else"

"I am not responsible for everybody else"

"I am not responsible for others problems"

"If I choose to assist another, I can now do so without harm to myself"

"It is safe to ... "

"It is easy to ..."

"It is fun to ..."

"I am ready to ..."

"I give myself permission to ..."

"I now willingly...learn from the past, live in the present, and plan for the future"

Recalibration Challenge Statement;

"This ... Chakra is now cleared and calibrated to the correct and appropriate frequency to enable optimal function and efficiency, safely, completely and easily."

Lessons from Case Histories.

Understanding how past incarnations affect the Psychic Body, here are some Case History tips.

Usually the Soul is given consideration for rest, consolidation and future planning between life-times, though at times in history this is not always possible, with some Souls working busily from one life time to the next, foregoing rest until certain aspects of their purpose have been achieved, or certain obstacles have been overcome. In this case, disillusionment can be an issue for that particular Soul.

Further considerations are:

- Planetary Planning, Cosmic Timing all come into this choice of present time incarnation.
- When timing is important for an incarnation – the window of opportunity presenting may be small, and the choices of and appropriate family to incarnate into may be limited:
- During times of upheaval or war not all events can be managed due to the varying nature of Souls "getting lessons" (or not) and the impact of their choices on outcomes: loose plans are laid – and have to be adapted as events unfold. Nothing is set in concrete, despite hopes for destiny.
- So if timing is important, a certain Plan "A" is a specific family / individual / place / culture, and a Plan "B" is also set up as fall-back in case the Soul has begun their preparation for journey into the womb/world, and unforeseen death has occurred in whatever form to the foetus or to the mother: the Soul may have to switch quickly to Plan "B" (Family "B") rather than hang around the same family for another opportunity. This

may cause its own type of scarring even before this incarnation;
- o If the incarnation is quick from one life time to the next, with little chance for full de-briefing, support, convalesce and resting for the Soul, the Soul may be struggling somewhat, but their mission /purpose usually helps keep them on "here" or on-track.
- o If the Soul has been counselled or "instructed" for a greater good to return quickly.
- o If a Soul needs to meet another Soul, and Soul has had to incarnate quickly.
- o If a mission has been aborted through unexpected death of self or host (chosen parent or foetal body / child's body).
- o Remember, plans can change as global consciousness "gets" some things that are necessary for fulfilment of a particular purpose, but may also not "get" something that is crucial, so another purpose is chosen, plans are shelved, or events are "waited-out".
- The Psychic Point can be invaded by others so check this for "in-out" energy settings, or whether there is a need to "seal" this area from inadvertent escapes.
- Inter-dimensional damage may affect the leg (Knee, Ankle, Mid-shins Chakras) function – possibly a Past Life memory triggered. In this case check the Spatial Chakras as well as other Master Centres.

MyRa SRi

PRIMARY POINTS

The following Primary Point suggestions are individually listed for each type or "group" of sensitivity or psychicness... Some people may find that they resonate with a more than one of these lists and may wish to check out a variety of suggestions for themselves. Mix and match as suits, as this is only a quick reference guide. And when in doubt, head to the page in *Balancing the Chakras* for the **Balance Sheet** – for a quick overview. Here are the groups or "types".

Sensitives and Empaths

Everything written here will be expanded for the Ultra-Sensitive. There is a difference between an Empath and a Sensitive, and it is usually connected with their Soul Journey and their stage of evolution.

Sensitives and Empaths both tend to absorb energy, though to varying degrees.

The Empath can feel and identify in order to assist. Usually when one is in the presence of someone or something that requires help. They may or may not "absorb" depending on their boundary level.

A Sensitive can also feel and identify, but they do not have to be next to the person to do so. Nor do they have to be in the same street or city... this all depends on their latent gifts, past-life experiences, past-life trainings, qualifications or Initiations and their chosen Soul Mission. Sometimes their sensitivity is meant to assist them in navigating energy and (in avoiding certain negative) people successfully, but this can also have been corrupted by some malign force at some historic point, and they may find instead of it being a gift, it has become a huge problem... Few experience this debility to such a degree, but I mention it as it is possible.

So navigating through energy by "tasting" or sampling it etherically in order to identify its safety quotient can be helpful. But when the same sensitivity leads to energy absorption, and one is unaware of it, it can create real problems. And may prevent progressing in certain areas.

This tendency to absorption is so important to understand.

Recognising the type of energy on some level is one thing, but actually absorbing it takes it to another level.

When it becomes entwined, intermingled with or etherically recorded on one's own energy systems, it can become harder to clear... it becomes resonant with one's own energy, and "hides" in the energy fields or Chakras. This can also compound to create film filters that prevent one from seeing clearly, as this low-grade absorbed energy interferes with one's vision.

Sure, it is a real gift to be able to know what another feels in order to assist them, but these unwanted and alien (not our own) energies are damaging if this then becomes (or overlays) how one feels or experiences or how one communicates.

Sensitive Primary Points

Once the total Psychic Chakra system has been balanced and cleared, there will be a clearer flow on incoming energies and the ability to interpret and process them.

Recognised, balanced, realigned and activated Sensory Psychic Chakras and a healthy Psychic Body will make life easier. However, I would recommend that during your week, you build in the exercises recommended to allow for a healthier tone. Particularly the Psychic Core Toner Meditation Exercise. (This is available for a few dollars at   ). This attention to your Psychic Body will also allow it to grow stronger and thus to protect you better. So whatever you do, ensure that you do this at the very least.

The Primary Points I would recommend to pay particular attention to – and this goes for energy workers or kinesiologists that have balanced the Psychic Chakras for a client and are having a follow-up session in which the Psychic Chakras are indicated as requiring attention – are as follows.

Best Chakras / Points to focus on for clearing, attention and realignment:

- The Spatial Chakras
- The Monitor Chakras
- Link Chakra
- Stability Chakra
- Solar Plexus Chakra
- Soul Star Chakra (above the head)
- 5th Earthing Chakra under the feet
- Soul Body Connection Point at the Navel

One could also quickly recheck the Shoulder Transducers, Causal Chakra and Core Star (for Soul body connection) and Soul Registration).

There may need to be mindfulness as to compatibility of energies with Sensitives. An Empathic will not be as thrown by someone else's energy that is not compatible with theirs, whilst a Sensitive can find the incompatibility creates such a dis-resonance with them that it causes a jarring in their energy fields. It is as though their Crystalline energy structure has been hammered, or set to a different rhythm. Their ability to respond and to be present shifts, so it is also worth paying some attention to the Crystalline body.

Some Ultra-Sensitives may need to check the more advanced Earthing Chakras, down to the 8th Earthing Chakra. We would also suggest a recheck of the Hara Line and Advanced Soul Body Anatomy as well as the condition of their Nadis and Gridding Systems. (These can be found in *"The New Evolved Chakras"* book or by doing the online course. Meditations on each of these are planned for release and publication asap – and may provide a cheaper solution.)

Empaths

Empaths could possibly follow the same list as for Sensitives. For some Empaths their boundaries may not be as compromised, the following list may serve well:

Empath Primary Points
- Stability Chakra
- Soul Star Chakra (above the head)
- 5th Earthing Chakra under the feet
- Soul Body Connection Point at the Navel
- Shoulder Transducers
- Causal Chakra and Core Star (for Soul body connection) and Soul Registration).

Psychics

Most problems I have observed for psychics centre around over-use of sensory Clair anatomy. Horn antennae are prone to get jammed in their fully open and alert position which is quite tiring and also makes it hard to find peace or relaxation time. Learning how to control and close down the Crown Chakra (and others) before bed can make a huge difference.

The "Chakra-Protect Meditation" guides you easily and safely through this process and is available through

or

Psychic Primary Points

The usual quick check places for Psychics are often around the head centres and head sensory anatomy, such as;

- The Horns Antennae
- Crown Chakra
- Ears, Eyes, Nose, Mouth Chakras
- Shoulder Transducers
- Spatial Chakras
- Stability Chakras
- Core Star

Also check connection points to Soul Body via Soul Star (8th Higher Chakra), soles of the Feet and 5th Earthing Chakra

Advanced Souls, Spiritual Journeyers

This group also includes healers, therapists, energy workers, Light Seekers.

Primary Points

The suggested points to focus on initially for any follow-up work could be:

- Thymus Chakra
- Causal Chakra
- Nose, Mouth and Third Eye/s Chakras
- Core Star
- Navel
- Knees Chakras
- Stability Chakra – Mid-Shins
- Sole of Feet
- Earthing Chakras
- Shoulder Transducers

But do feel free to start anywhere. Follow your intuition and inner knowing. Things will reveal themselves as you work with your Sensory apparatus anyway, no matter where you begin.

The Conscious, Aware and Those challenged by Energetic Contamination or Challenges.

I would suggest that you start initially with the Crown Chakra and Core Star.

When these are cleared and balanced, go to any Chakra or Point that feels appropriate – you can do this by scanning the outer space of the head and body to see / feel which area requires initial attention. You may also choose to follow any of the other group's Primary Points as outlined.

Light Seekers and Conscious Souls working towards Mastery

Go to any Chakra or Point that feels appropriate – you can do this by scanning the outer space of the head and body to see / feel which area requires initial attention. You may also choose to follow any of the other group's Primary Points as outlined.

If you are consciously working towards Mastery, I can suggest the following;

Primary Points
- Transpersonal Chakra
- Back of the Neck Chakra
- Throat Chakra
- Eye Chakras
- Shoulder Transducers
- Spatial Chakras

NOTE:
If you are not sure which group you are, just look at the pictures and illustrations and test (kinesiology or dowsing) or intuit (or inner knowing) to those which feel unresolved or unclear.

As you clear and strengthen the alignments in your Sensory apparatus, you will become quicker at ascertaining what and where your attention needs to go.

BALANCE - SUMMARY

INCLUDES:

BALANCING THE CHAKRAS

BALANCE – CORRECTION SHEET

SUMMARY – TOWARD EVOLUTION

PUTTING IT ALL TOGETHER

BALANCING THE CHAKRAS

IDENTIFY IMBALANCE

If you are able, you can ascertain what current status the individual Chakra is at then recheck after your correction or balance;

1. POSITION (angle, slipped, or correct position)
2. POLARITY (positive, negative, neutral OR input, output, frozen)
3. Not currently part of the individual's anatomy (depending on their star-birth-right / identity & purpose) – not yet mature / not yet required for this life journey
4. Not present / repressed / sublimated / suppressed / hiding – not yet activated
5. Present but not matured / not evolved / or has been devolved
6. Not functioning / not activated / "switched off"
7. Blocked / congested / overwhelmed
8. Damaged / injured / broken
9. Off kilter / off-"orbit" / misaligned / twisted
10. Previous balances not registered, accepted or aligned with the Soul of the Being
11. Psychic Control Gate interference or control or Soul not fully present

This last point can indicate control by another, or the Soul not fully housed in the body (due to shock, fear, avoidance etc) and requires support to re-enter/ re-commit to enter

Condition of Chakra

Assess the condition; Chakras can become cloudy, twisted, disfigured, torn, bent, blocked or have a part of its anatomy loosened from its nesting place.

You can gather more information if required by assessing the **before** balance and **after** balance conditions of any Chakra you are working with...

- Colour
- Tone
- Spin
- Texture
- Freedom Of Movement
- 100% Clear Of Interference Of Blockages Or Other Mechanism / Intent
- 100% Availability To One's Self Alone
- 100% Optimal Functionality
- Any Messages?
- Any Old Stories Requiring Attention / Resolution
- Correctly connected to the Psychic body anatomy as a whole

BALANCE or CORRECTION SHEET

Some Suggested Ideas;

1. Balance:
    a. Oils
    b. Colour, / Colour Shower
    c. Symbols
    d. Client Journey exploration
    e. Karmic Release – self or another's
    f. Male / Female Alignment
    g. Earthing Chakra Alignment
    h. Other
2. Alignment and activation of Chakra required
3. Filter requires cleaning
4. Sound / An Affirmation or Challenge Statement
5. Release of implants, devices etc
6. Removal of previous Seals, Sigils etc
7. Release of injunction, Auric net, any other interference or link
8. Scan by priority to cross-balance Chakra To Chakra
9. LeyLine interference / impact
10. If Psychic Control Point; clear Controller hook / imprint / energy; or confirm that Soul is willing to return - Assist, and then Seal
11. Frequency, spin or orbit requires adjustment or Recalibration
12. Ancient / Other Issue arresting Chakra initiation

PSYCHIC Chakra Balance Notes:

....
....
....
....
....
....
....
....
....
....
....
....
....
....
....
....
....
....
....
....
....
....
....
....

TOWARD EVOLUTION NOT EGO

As is obvious by now, our evolving subtle body anatomy has undergone quite some changes over the years.

We appear to be in the midst of further changes still, as we hold our ground and continue to hold the Light. There are still some challenges to be had and some tests to be passed or overcome. For some, this is part of their Soul purpose and journey and part of the mission here. It hasn't been easy and we may not fully reap of the rewards, but we are at the Coal-face, if you like, actually being part of the shifts and changes and in the long run, this is something that cannot be experienced or understood any other way than by full and complete participation.

Working with the New Evolved Chakras assists our own evolution, and it helps us house and hold a higher vibrationary light. This is essential, as going Out-There To Change The World does not necessarily automatically mean that we are changing or holding the light within. For we can get caught up with the agenda of other things, or of others or allow too much energy of others to interfere. Finding the balance is so important, for we may find that without it, we also run the risk of an enlarged or out of control ego.

Having seen others engage in certain supposed spiritual processes and then claiming to be enlightened does not convince me that they have actually attained that position. Reaching enlightenment on certain points of understanding or appreciation doesn't necessarily equate to full enlightenment. And claiming to personally be an Enlightened One certainly gives me cause to doubt the truth of the statement. I do not think a truly Enlightened Being needs to (or would even claim to) state that that is who or what they are. The term Evolving sits more readily with me, as it is a process, and from here I cannot fully yet see what I am evolving into, though I may dare to hazard a guess or two. Keeping the highest and purest intent is the only way to evolve correctly, or the ego can turn it into a *de*volving.

I feel this current anatomy will serve us well for quite some years, and may actually be all we need to know for some time about the new energy anatomy and Chakras. Be assured I will keep my ears to the wind for further updates if they should emerge in my remaining years. In the words of techno-speak, we now have upgrades well into the next couple of Generations.

Astral Travel

Clients have asked me about this so I include more on it here as over the last twenty years the astral landscape has really changed.

So, a word of warning about Astral Travel. Glamorous as it seems, there was a time when it was reasonably safe to embark on such interesting journeys. Indeed I did so myself from time to time. I have since learned by experience that things are no longer the same, and with the plethora of inter-dimensional beings and astral entities currently flitting and engaging between worlds and spheres at this time in Earth history, it is much riskier than it used to be. Certain other metaphysicians besides myself and others I consider of great wisdom also now advise against it. If you wish to take the gamble, there is nothing to stop you, but I would ask you to be aware that to do so will put you at much greater risk than you may possibly realise. Seeking your true Spiritual Source may hopefully give you the spiritual and etheric satisfaction you seek without the same danger.

Spiritual Power, Not Force

Psychic – Sensory – Spiritual – Gifted – Sensitive – Aware – Empath…. Which are you?

Here are some of my thoughts on the subject.

To achieve the best results with the information in this book, it is always best to by-pass the astral plane, the spirits, the etheric, the pseudo-psychic, power-hungering and –mongering and only seek the highest Divine that you possibly can. In the Divine there can be seen darkness – one only has to read the bible to know that there is an angry and a jealous God out there – but in the True Divine there is no Darkness. Rather than seek personalities, power-beings, Masters or Gurus, seek to embrace your inner knowing and Higher Self and reach to your Highest and Purest Light manifestation and access. This will guarantee you no karma from using any psychic talents for spiritual ends.

I have seen Masters of psychic powers, manipulators of laws and energy, who channel in the dark without realizing it, and this taints not only their work and their "patients" but also their karma. In healing we must break away from the old model of using psychism for power or gain and engage in the right use of it – for good, the benefit of all. Whilst being paid for our time and energy is a right of every practitioner.

To be Spiritual is so much more important than to have flashy psychic gifts or to know all the correct language and quotes, or to be able to spew forth the latest spiritual "buzz" words on command. Walking the "talk" of working with the Light is the true challenge and proof of one's integrity and spirituality.

I will also issue a warning here, one that I usually teach in the Spiritual-Protection-HygienEthics class; Do not go checking psychically into another person's business or affairs **without** *invitation*, or unless they are negatively impacting on you directly. It is none of your business. Just as the act of them checking into you, into your mind, into your thoughts or into what you are doing is none of their business. If they are playing with or holding any aspect of dark, or going through difficult times, or are of an inharmonious vibration, or if they have a negative entity on them, you will soon enough know about it because it will knock your own Psychic Body and system around, and create problems for you. So clear these off and out and keep your affairs separate. If you are in the habit of letting your mind wander into the affairs of others, this will leave you open to others wandering into your personal business.

I counsel that unless requested to do so or for your own personal protection, don't open up to another's personal business for there is also a possibility that you will also be opening portals to whatever it is that they are dealing with or doing.

Don't.Do.It! Please!

Make sure that when you think of someone that when you cease thinking about them, you *close* down that space and that mental or energetic opening.

Practice Spiritual-Cleansing (or Protection-HygienEthics) if you get hit this way. There are some ideas for this in my book *"Secrets Behind Energy Fields"*.

To rephrase something mentioned earlier; not everyone has all of these Chakras fully present or yet ready.

Most of us possess these unique aspects of the new Psychic Chakras and their subtle body connections and functions or most of us *will* possess them eventually.

But their presence or the possibility for full activation and function will also depend on the Soul identity, essence, character, journey and mission for each being or person. The spiritual calibre so to speak. And this will decide the requirement of that which they may need.

Our job, if you like, should we be called to facilitate or energy work, is to assist the presenting Soul with the technology and knowhow to help them activate these present and current centres appropriately, whilst being also aware that results may also be dependent on the Soul's present capacity for these new Chakras and connections.

This does not necessarily mean that if a Chakra is not showing right now, that it won't show up at all. It just may be a matter of time, or of further processing, or even simply more new energy light frequencies emerging as we travel through the Galaxy that will give them the extra oomph or boost to their next stage. Meanwhile, you are now equipped and have knowledge and an understanding to handle issues in this area.

Congratulations!

It has been a pleasure to share with you and journey with you. I wish you well in your explorations.

May you find more Light and freedom through opening to your new Chakras.

MyRa SRi

PUTTING IT ALL TOGETHER

We trust that you have gained some understanding of the benefits and the functions of the Sensory Chakras, and of how they can enhance and assist with our progress in the new Era, and with our Sensitive clients.

We have had the opportunity to align with some of these Chakras as we have progressed through the pages, even before beginning work on them. At certain points there have been references to specific ways of working with and balancing some of these Chakras.

We have covered the requirements of correct alignment and energetic preparation *before* commencing any accurate energetic work with the new Chakra system that I doubt has been covered anywhere else. (I could be wrong, but we personally are not aware of these anywhere else.) We have included illustrations of the clearing for the Light Channel in the head, the Central Core Channel and for the clearing of Filters and Blocks.

We have also become familiar with *Tools for Working with the Chakras* - for both the therapist and the self-journeyer to utilise.

Affirmations (also used as Statements of Challenge) have assisted us to trigger and navigate through various histories, stories and consciousnesses of a Chakra in order to ensure integrity.

Colour or Essence infusion or Essential Oils suggestions have assisted in correcting or infusing appropriate vibrational frequencies.

Soul Registration protocol has been provided. Changes and shifts have begun or been concluded along the way.

In short, we trust that *now* you are not quite the same person that *began* reading this book, but a more balanced, supported and confident Sensitive, Empath or Soul Journeyer and Human being.

It has been my privilege to share this new information with you.

We wish you well on your spiritual journey.

Be Well, Stay Well, and Blessings

Myra Sri

Further Information

The New Evolved Chakras

The Sensory Psychic Chakra system covered in this book is from the New Chakra Balancing Training series. The series is all about The New Evolved Chakras Systems for this era. These include two other vital systems – The New Earthing Chakras, and the Signal / Survival Chakras – as well as up to date information on the Advancements in Soul Body anatomy, Nadis and Gridding Systems. These all interlink and are vital to navigate through issues and the world's energy at large at this time and for the foreseeable future. To learn more about these you can get the book or register interest for further information on the online course.

Questions and Contact Information

Please feel free to write to the Author with your success stories. Your questions are welcomed and every endeavour will be made to answer each one. This book has been compiled through long and personal journeying, personal experience whilst researching, and through teaching and practicing in consultancy. It also attempts to answer the needs of clients and energy workers.

If you would like more information about this or any other book or meditation or to be kept informed on any further publications, you can email her direct, or register your email for newsletters at www.myrasri.com

Or follow Myra at her Amazon Author page:

Colour Images

To assist the reader with energy balancing, colour images and charts are available for the genuine print book-buyer upon request. The New Sensitive Sensory Psychic Chakras Workbook with full colour images will also be ready soon.

For further information, kindly email

If there is anything more you wish to know about, then **YOU** are invited to contact me with your most burning questions as to the subject of this book or regarding energy, life, relationships, depression, self-identity or self-help, self-individuation, self-development or responsibility.

In return, your questions will be answered and when there are enough questions, a free copy of any resulting new book will be sent to you as a "Thank You"!

To send your question or comments, email:

About the Author

With over thirty years knowledge, study and practice in the energy and esoteric fields, and a lifetime's experience as an Indigo Sensitive, Myra Sri now documents the profound shifts and changes in the human esoteric and subtle body anatomy. As a trainer, teacher and energy practitioner, Myra has been developing and teaching Advanced Energy Healing and Kinesiology courses since the mid Nineties.

Sharing her new discoveries and research over the last sixteen years, she endeavours to explain the impacts of the current energy shifts experienced around the globe, especially on the energy bodies of humanity. Documenting the updates with new Chakras, the Soul Body, the Nadis and our current Energy Gridding Systems Myra focuses in particular on the Sensory Psychic Chakras and anatomy and New Evolved Chakras.

Ground-breaking work and a labour of love, she has included tools, diagrams and affirmations outlined to assist the genuine journeyer to balance, align and manage their new anatomy and to enhance the Soul's journey toward Ascension or their own individual evolution. Energy Healers and workers wondering why balances do not hold, especially when working with trauma clients, soul-damaged beings, the psychically challenged and the earth healer-worker may well find answers in the New Evolved Psychic Chakras that makes sense and is practical.

Invaluable information on maintaining oneself in these transforming and climactic times that has not been revealed elsewhere.

THE NEW EVOLVED CHAKRAS

Available on Amazon and online bookstores. Or order direct from the author: admin@myrasri.com

THE ENERGY HEALING SECRETS SERIES

www.ingramcontent.com/pod-product-compliance
Lightning Source LLC
Chambersburg PA
CBHW050536300426
44113CB00012B/2132